From fear to *flow*

From fear to *flow*

PETER SHEARER

Drawn from the wisdom of science, psychology, Eastern and Western philosophy and the martial arts, this highly engaging guide will help you move beyond fear-based limitations to the state of flow.

From Fear To Flow

2nd edition, published 2022 by Peter Shearer

First published 2020 as *Embrace Fear, Find Flow* by Peter Shearer

Copyright © Peter Shearer 2022

The moral rights of the author have been asserted.

All rights reserved. No part of this publication may be reproduced, stored in a retrieval system, or transmitted in any form or by any means electronic, mechanical, photocopying, recording or otherwise without written permission of the publisher and the copyright holder.

Cover by U.T. and Riddhish Chanda
Internal design by Zena Shapter
Original artwork by Olivia Case

Typeset in Georgia and Lucinda

*This book is dedicated to the loves and lights of my life.
Janine, Zac and Jessica.*

We can not expect anyone to help us live; we must discover how to do it by ourselves. To 'live' means; to live in fullness, without waste of time or potential, expressing one's uniqueness, yet participating ultimately in the complexity of the cosmos.

Finding Flow – Mihaly Csikszentmihalyi

The cave you fear to enter holds the treasure you seek.

Joseph Campbell

Contents

Acknowledgements	11
Foreword	13
Chapter 1: From fear to flow	15
Chapter 2: How does fear do its thing? The chemistry of fear	27
Chapter 3: Rewiring your 'firing' – the 'how to' of changing behaviours	46
Chapter 4: The humble (though highly valuable) pause button	51
Chapter 5: Fears, beliefs and behaviours	60
Chapter 6: The dance of consciousness	73
Chapter 7: Being present – achieving mindfulness	83
Chapter 8: Embracing fear	100
Chapter 9: Reframing	109
Chapter 10: Learning to centre – creating a dynamic stillness	122
Chapter 11: Additional principles and practices from the martial arts	139
Chapter 12: Distinctions between Western and Eastern thought	153
Chapter 13: Flow – the Western view	164
Chapter 14: Flow – the Eastern view	185
Chapter 15: Zen	209
Chapter 16: The geometry of conflict	224
Chapter 17: A model to remember: CCE	237
Chapter 18: A few thoughts about luck	241
Chapter 19: The hero's journey	246
Notes/Bibliography	271
About the Author	279

Acknowledgements

This book began in 2014 and was first published under the title 'Embrace fear, find flow' in 2020. Since this first publication, I have made thousands of edits to the original book, which include changing the title, adding new information, downsizing in some areas and a complete cover-to-cover rewrite of the content. Over this extended period of time, covering the production of both books, I have been most fortunate to have had the support of a wonderful collection of family, friends, mentors and experts. I would first like to thank, from my heart and soul, my beautiful wife Janine, who has been unrelenting in her support and encouragement for this project. I have greatly benefitted from your unfiltered truths, clear insights and contribution on so many levels – in particular when my writing experience was anything but flow. You have been with me on every paragraph of this book. To my son Zac and daughter Jessica, I acknowledge you both for the belief you have shown in me and your unconditional love and support. To Tarryn Mallick, my first Editor. Your perceptive insights, honesty and talent really helped me move through and beyond the struggles I experienced with my first drafts. To Patrick Buckley, my second Editor; it has been a blast working with you and I have greatly appreciated your capacity to understand the spirit which weaves through the narrative of this book.

To Professor Rufus Black, who has kindly written the Foreword. Thank you for introducing me to the profound work of Mihaly Csikszentmihalyi many years ago and for being such a talented, warm-hearted and inspiring human being. To my fine friends Matt Murdoch and Danielle Aitken, I salute you both for your wise insights and very generous help. To Olivia Case, the artist. I am deeply appreciative of the paintings and drawings you have contributed to this book. They really capture the vibrant spirit of flow. To Sensei's Tamaki and Tokashiki of Okinawa – thank you both for your guidance and wisdom and for the inspiring ability to make the flow state visible in karate. I would also like to thank Tony Carroll. For four decades you have been my Karate-do mentor and great friend. I have been most fortunate to have you as a constant compass point in the Martial Arts. May the 'do' continue to be our path in the decades to come.

I would also like to extend my deep gratitude to Michael Rennie for your brilliance and tenacity and for being such a visionary. To Sarah Tansey, Regan Forde and Kristie Overs, I extend a huge thank you for your generous guidance in helping me navigate through the nuances (and perils) of the English language. To my brother Rob and sister Annette, thank you for your constant love and support. Finally, a huge thanks to the highly competent and creative, fellow author, Zena Shapter, who has been brilliant in guiding this book's process from the final edit through to full publication.

Foreword

Writing this foreword is an opportunity for a moment of gratitude.

Years ago, when I was at McKinsey & Company, I had the privilege of working with Peter. We were preparing for a workshop with the senior team of a leading Australian company that was seeking to transform its culture. We were introducing them to concepts from Western thought and research, including ideas like the notion of flow, which could help them to lead in new ways consistent with the sort of culture they were looking to create. We had some interesting exercises to help them that came from contemporary psychological research. These worked well enough, but they didn't reach everyone and we had a sense that deeper engagement was possible.

Peter paused and said he had some thoughts about some other ways we could engage them coming out of his martial arts experience. I had always admired those with martial arts skills. I had done a little Taekwon-Do as a teenager and understood that for those who journeyed far in those traditions, it was as much about mind as body, indeed the physical actions were an expression of mind.

Peter took us through a series of ideas and, importantly, exercises around being centred and creating flow in the way of the Japanese martial art Aikido. Peter is a compelling teacher as you will discover in this book. Those lessons that I learnt that day – and which I have been exploring the meaning of ever since because they are those kinds of lessons – have been some of the most important in shaping how I lead. They have served me well both personally and professionally. They are ideas I have found that I end up explaining to colleagues and friends although never as well as Peter explained them that first time. They are ideas that have become an integral part of my personal philosophy of life. Thank you, Peter.

Many of these ideas Peter explores in this book are ones that I have found invaluable over the years, from guiding my own life to leading organisations. Rarely is there a week that goes by when I don't think about where I am sitting in relation to being in a state of flow and making adjustments to try to stay closer to being in that spot. Through challenging times and tasks, that question has been key to navigating through and staying well.

One of the privileges of working with Peter is seeing him in action in workshops where he covers the sorts of ideas in this book here. The experience of reading this book is very like being in a workshop with Peter. He brings transformed ideas to life with personal stories, memorable visual pictures of them and clear explanations of ideas that you would otherwise need to read a whole book to discover. Best of all, there is a practical edge to all that Peter explores here. I hope you enjoy the journey with Peter as much as I have.

Professor Rufus Black
Vice Chancellor of the University of Tasmania

Chapter 1:
From fear to flow

The recognition was immediate. If I didn't move and do it quickly, I would be shortly crushed by a rolling wall of water. As the moment unfolded, I was caught in a tension between two powerful emotional forces. One of fear, the other excitement and both were wrestling for primacy.

A short time before I had been languidly paddling on my wave ski past the line of beach breaks to watch some top-class surfers take on the massive waves which were peeling off the bombora at Long Reef, on the Northern Beaches of Sydney. My plan was to sit out on the far edge of the waves and enjoy the action, from a safe distance. I soon arrived at this 'edge' but continued to paddle, closer to the impact zone. Within a few moments I was within metres of where the waves surged off the bombora, feeling awe-struck and exhilarated by being so close to such powerful expressions of nature.

These waves, which I could almost reach out and touch, were double the size of anything I had surfed before. Though extremely exciting, I instinctively knew it was not safe to stay here as a rogue wave could easily hit. The decision was simple. Paddle to the right and I would quickly find safe waters. A couple of strokes to the left and I would be in the direct path of a few rolling tonnes of unbridled nature. Fear was ringing all the alarm bells but, for some reason, I didn't respond.

I surrendered to the call of the wild man within and paddled left, into the rising lip of a monster and joined with it. Once I had made the decision, all emotion departed. I felt no fear or excitement. Instead, I was consumed by a sense of calm, a stillness which stayed with me through the entirety of that magical ride. (*When I close my eyes now, many years after the event, I can still sense the wave rising beneath me and see the blue curve rolling me within it*). As I eventually steered off the wave, momentum caused me to become airborne. For a moment, I soared sunward, just long enough to register the ecstatic feeling of flight before gravity returned me to the wide, blue ocean beneath with a resounding thump. On landing, I triumphantly thrust my paddle to the heavens, shouting out my many thanks to Poseidon and his entourage and then heard a sound I had never heard before, and will never hear again. This was the applause and loud cheers of local surfers who had witnessed my ride and who, for a moment, had given up their animosity to an unwelcome 'Goat Boater'. I then settled back and let the wash of emotion rush over me. The feeling was an overwhelming sense of excitement and elation. I slowly paddled back to shore and in those few quiet moments, had time to reflect on what I had just experienced. The ride had been pure joy. Years later, I came to realise it was also pure 'flow.'[1]

This story, though just a simple tale of surfing, captures both the guiding spirit of this book as well as the central theme. This theme is represented by the interplay between fear and the self-preserving role it plays, balanced against all those other aspects of life which call to you from the edge of your comfort zone.

If fear is allowed too much influence and prominence, it will cripple the fullness of your life. The cost is simple to identify. Tally up the lost opportunities. They will be especially salient in areas such as career, relationships, creativity and adventure. Over decades of working with people and seeing, firsthand, how fear can diminish, derail, even destroy lives, I was inspired to write this book. Fear is not the enemy, however. The challenge is developing a healthy relationship with this powerful emotion, so that fear fulfils its noble purpose of protecting you and, at the same time, you are still able to live a bountiful life. This book is designed to help you achieve this connection and create the foundations in life to experience higher levels of happiness, fulfilment and *flow*.

There are two key approaches which set this book or guide apart from others. One is the strategy which advocates engagement with fear, hence the title. Central to this approach is the avoidance of trying to deny, override or resist the sway of this emotion. Putting it simply, fear needs to be *embraced*. The other key approach is to draw upon a range of contributing sources from the sciences, Eastern and Western philosophy and the martial arts to create a broad set of practical tools to deal with fear. The breadth of this approach is critical. Attempting to deal with fear using only a psychological approach fails to recognise the interplay between the body and the mind and the way fear manifests. Similarly, to use just a somatic approach will fail to uncover the root cause as to why it shows up, when it does, particularly when it is not needed or warranted. It is best to have a range of tools on hand, as your personal Department of Fear is very influential, widely networked and has gained immense experience over the eons of evolution.

This powerful emotion is very deserving of our appreciation, after all it is driven by a singular and noble purpose. This raison d'etre lies in keeping you alive. Fear is not some malicious, life-limiting entity inhabiting your psyche, attempting to make your life miserable and restricted. When it fires up, it is essentially a series of chemical reactions, responding to a situation which has been perceived by your brain to be a threat. The fight or flight mechanism is activated within your limbic system and you react. In the initial stages of a reaction, your brain does not take the time out to discern whether the threat is genuine. Ensuring your safety is the impelling and automatic driver of this process.

This capacity to launch out of danger's way is a brilliant piece of systems engineering (when it is activated in moments of genuine threat). We will go into detail around this in later chapters. The real focus of this guide is to enable you to work with fear when you have discretion regarding how much you interpret something – an action, event or someone – as threatening. Jumping to avoid a tiger snake a moment before you tread on it is a very threatening, fear-inducing event and one which does not allow for discretion in how you react. However, if next week's meeting with a senior leader has caused you to feel anxious and fear has taken up residence, rent free, in your psyche, you *do* have discretion around how you interpret and respond to this situation and the fear that it is causing. With mindfulness and the application of some simple techniques, presented in the following chapters, you can reduce the levels of stress and fear generated by such everyday events as dealing with authority figures.

Research has shown us that when experiencing fear there are two different biological patterns which guide your responses. One is passive and based around your memories, innate predispositions and social context. The other is active, which gives you the opportunity to choose how you interpret what is happening to you and what your response will be.[2] If your usual manner of responding is the former, 'passive', then you will default to your established patterns of behaviour. These could include counter-attacking with sarcasm or dialling it up further and being physically aggressive in the face of a threat. These responses are passive, as you are following deeply embedded patterns. You are not reflecting upon the options before you, but just reacting. A stimulus occurs – a negative comment directed towards you – and you immediately default to a tried and trusted reaction. You bite back with an even more caustic comment. Other options in terms of how you could respond are not considered.

If you take an 'active' position however, you are open to exploring and applying a range of responses. In the example given, a constructive response could be used to try and resolve whatever is causing the negativity. This active approach is given great prominence in this guide for it highlights a way forward for you to make conscious, constructive and life-affirming choices in any moment, in any situation. It is a tool for personal growth which can be used and reused daily. This tool is highly adaptable, never wears out or suffers from overuse or irrelevance. It was the ancient Greeks who first illuminated the significance of controlling impulse as a way of shaping character. In contemporary psychological terms it applies to the capacity to self-regulate, to consciously choose your response to external stimuli.

Taking an active approach to fear means shaping a relationship with this emotion whereby it is more of a companion (and occasional helpful warning light) and less of a control agent or even worse, a dictator to be obeyed. To get there you will need a healthy dose of self-awareness, access to courage and a willingness to welcome some new mindsets and minor disciplines into your day-to-day life. Changing your relationship with fear will amount to a reset in parts of your life. This will require letting go of unhelpful patterns of thinking, including some of the stories you tell yourself which are demeaning and have outlived their relevance. Failing to land the lead role in your kindergarten play shouldn't put the brakes on pursuing a thespian career twenty years down the path. At a critical juncture in my life, had I listened to my own very vocal and opinionated inner critic, the career I have enjoyed over the last three decades would not have eventuated.

My career trajectory has been a somewhat irregular one. I started out as a high school humanities teacher, then explored the human potential movement and taught self-development programs, and finally culminated as a consultant working for an international firm. In this later career I have operated as a facilitator and coach and have worked in over thirty countries. I specialised in the areas of leadership development and organisational culture change and have had the pleasure of engaging with thousands of individuals ranging from the Board and executive positions through to the front line.

One ever present dynamic which intrigued me over this tenure and inspired this guide, was the impact that fear had upon the lives of the people I was working with. Too frequently I have witnessed intelligent, capable and creative individuals hide their light. Often self-described as lacking confidence, these people would live out a pattern of playing small and take on the psyche of an 'Imposter'. This is someone who feels they do not 'belong' in some organisation or group and are destined to be found out and shown the door, sooner or later. Self-protection and keeping a low profile are completely understandable when confronted by bullying; however, this was rarely the case, as this pattern of playing 'less than' showed up in everyday interactions such as during meetings, conversations or presentations. Opportunities would surface – a chance to share their views or to challenge a decision (and significantly for some, openings for promotion) – and they would remain mute. These missed opportunities were usually followed by frustration and anger directed at self. As a coach I found these situations highly intriguing. I was working with self-aware, intelligent professionals who could easily play back to me the downside of their behaviours, but frequently felt powerless to navigate a way out of these limiting patterns. In drilling down to pure cause and effect, fear in some form always emerged. Fear of being judged and rejected, fear of getting it wrong, fear of standing out, fear of challenging authority and on and on... Insight is helpful, but for real progress the way out of such inhibiting patterns is to unpack them, understand the actual 'drivers' of such behaviours and plan a set of actions in order to make progress. This requires facing up to some hard truths. Like Dante's Inferno, the way out of hell is through it and individuals wishing to transform their relationship with fear need to steer into it. This guide is designed to help this process by providing quality information and a variety of tools, skills and techniques that are well tested, wide ranging and highly practical. The rewards for moving beyond such limitations are the broadening of possibilities and the opportunity to experience greater levels of fun, fulfilment and flow.

So how to move from fear to flow? Our initial step is to first understand what flow is and why it is worth seeking out. This exploration of flow will be through two distinct perspectives, one drawing from Eastern philosophy, the other from the West. The following paragraphs are to serve as an abridged synopsis of the subject. In later chapters we go into far greater levels of depth on what flow is and how you can experience more of it in your life.

Finding flow – Western view

At the forefront of research into flow is a Hungarian/American legend by the name of Mihalyi Csikszentmihalyi – pronounced "chik-sent-me high". He has been a scientist and researcher for over five decades, wedded to a personal mission to understand what it is that enables people to be at their best... to be in flow. What a fabulous way to spend fifty years! Unfortunately, he left the planet in 2021 and in the wake of his passing, humanity lost one of its great champions. Into his eighties, he continued to research and expand on what was already a prodigious body of work. At its centre was his quest to understand flow, which he defines as;

> 'A state when people are performing at their best and are fully engaged in what they are doing and loving it.' [3]

This experience is also similarly described as being in the 'Zone'.

You have experienced flow before. Somewhere on a sporting field where everything just seemed to click, leading a presentation when your words streamed effortlessly, creating music where all the parts just coalesced in perfect harmony, or you may have found yourself deep in a rich, engaging conversation, fully absorbed in the moment. Children frequently demonstrate the flow state. Observe them in play and see their lack of self-consciousness, their full engagement in what they are doing and their absorption in the moment.

You experience flow more frequently than you realise. You don't need to be Beyoncé in front of a million fans, striving for that final high note, or Michelangelo about to apply a master brushstroke. To experience more of the flow state requires you to initially learn how to be consciously present. Meaning your mind is fully in the present moment and nowhere else. Once presence becomes more of a norm, the next step is to deal with whatever impedes you from being fully and enjoyably immersed in whatever you are doing, as you are doing it. The usual culprits are a hyperactive mind or fear in some form. Other derailers include an excessive need for control, being bored, lazy or being permanently stuck in your comfort zone. In the chapters to come, you will be shown how to move beyond such limitations and engage more effortlessly with the state of flow.

Eastern view

In the East, flow is synonymous with the natural world, in particular the element of water. This association is found in some of the finest texts from the Orient including, the 'I Ching' and 'Tao Te Ching'. Water always finds the lowest point to rest. It supports all life and though 'humble,' over time it can wear away mountains and destroy steel. It also has a way of conserving energy by adapting and shaping itself to the contours around it. Such characteristics endeared Eastern philosophers to this element and helped it become a revered symbol and an inspiration to those seeking to experience flow and ultimately spiritual illumination. Be like water, the great texts suggest. Be humble, be supportive of those around you and wherever you may be, find the lowest point to build your energy. And when ready, allow yourself to move forward, following the contours of the life around you, not imposing yourself on it.

The Eastern appreciation of flow is also found deeply ingrained in the healing arts such as acupuncture and shiatsu as well as expressed through the martial arts, most evidently in tai chi. The beautiful flowing movements of this ancient art reflects the natural state of water. Effortless action. Flow.

My initial exposure to Eastern philosophy began when I took my first steps inside a karate dojo. This was the beginning of a love affair I have had with the art now for over forty years.

In karate-do, an important milestone is achieved in the earning of one's first black belt. When this happened to me, my Japanese Sensei described, in unflattering terms and with a bemused smile; "*Your karate is very rigid ... like a block of ice ...* (this is all he said at first followed by an extended pause. He just looked at me for what seemed a long time and then finally continued) *... No movement, no flow ... Like ice you have to melt, first at the edges ... this has to happen before you can flow.*"

His observations, though rather painful for my twenty-year-old ego, who just for a moment was trying to feel good about achieving my first black belt, were both prescient and wise. His analogy has continued to serve me well over the decades as I am still learning to relax, soften and find my flow effortlessly. My intention is that this guide will help you *melt* around the edges and find your flow state.

Some guidelines

The information presented in the following chapters is structured in three major sections: Mindfulness, Finding Centre and Flow. Being mindful or present refers to when the mind and body are in a unified state and when you physically feel you are fully in the moment and nowhere else. I will be using the words mindful and presence interchangeably throughout this guide. Becoming present is the first step towards being centred. When you are centred you feel resourceful and connected with life around you and the life force within you. The final state is flow – this is where you are fully engaged in a meaningful activity unhindered by distractions or negative thoughts. There is an effortlessness to your actions, and you experience yourself at your best. Flow can be observed watching the masterful Roger Federer in full flight or even Trevor, your neighbour, at the weekend tennis comp. Most likely Roger will experience more flow than Trevor, as he has learnt to quieten the inner narrative, be present and engage fully. Trevor's attention unfortunately is too widely dispersed as he tries to impress onlookers, whilst simultaneously indulging his inner critic.

Being mindful – Learning to centre – Finding flow

The framework below sets out the structure of this guide. At the top level, as mentioned, are the three major subject areas;

- Being Mindful

- Learning to Centre

- Finding Flow

Under these core areas there are a variety of subsections designed to help make the information more user friendly.

- 🧰 *Toolbox*: Highlights specific skills, techniques or tools you can use in your personal and professional life.

- 👜 *Exercises*: Activities to help you apply the skills, techniques and tools presented.

- *So what?* Answers the question; Why is this piece of information important?

- *Tips*: Identifies an unusual or unexpected use or application of the tools.

- *Reflection*: A strong suggestion to pause and reflect upon what is being presented.

- *Case Studies:* These are stories which illustrate the real-life use of the tools, techniques and approaches covered in this guide.

We start with the bigger picture, the What and the Why and then drill down to the How. The purpose of this structure is to keep the flow of information ordered and interconnected and ultimately shaped towards practical application. The skills, tools and exercises presented can be effectively applied in both the personal and professional spheres of life and what is offered in these pages has been born out of lived experience. In terms of the writing approach, I frequently draw upon stories, metaphors and analogies. The use of such literary devices helps cut through complexity and is intended to deliver information in a memorable, concise and creative manner. And finally, I frequently use the term mind/body. The point behind this is to avoid distinguishing between either mind or body as they are both acting in concert with each other.

> *Body and mind seem like two separate entities but have actually been proven to be one and the same.*[4]

Another more poetic expression of this connection is to do with the manner in which the mind is not just located in the head, but;

> *'... travels the whole body on caravans of hormone and enzyme, busily making sense of the compound wonders we catalogue as touch, taste, hearing and vision.'*[5]

So, let's begin. Our next step is to explore what fear is, what causes it and what makes up its biochemistry.

Disclaimer

This guide is not intended as a substitute for medical or other professional care. If you suffer from any significant condition associated with fear, particularly over a longer term, then seek professional help. Though the exercises in this guide may help with conditions associated with fear, there are no definitive claims as such.

Chapter 2:
How does fear do its thing? The chemistry of fear.

What flows through your mind, sculpts your brain.

Rick Hanson PhD.

The audience was full of energy and anticipation. The MC hushed the room and began his warm welcome to the next presenter ... me. I was inexperienced at public speaking being in my mid-twenties, but I felt confident as I walked towards the stage. I knew my material well. As the podium neared, I made a slight alteration to the order of my presentation. I climbed the few steps to the podium and started to become conscious of a low gradient of fear stirring in my stomach. Whether it was my last-minute decision to alter my presentation or the reality of all that attention focused on me, fear was gradually making its presence felt. I remember an increasing level of discomfort in my gut. I was experiencing more than just 'butterflies' – these ones fluttered with attitude. By the time I had settled my notes on the podium, smiled my first smile at the large, silent, expectant group, a mini war had erupted within me. This small discomfort in my gut had now grown into a sizable beast and was looking to expand its turf. My higher mind, in its more evolved manner, was sending signals to put on a brave face, exude confidence and override this fear. A core emotion like fear, however, having had millions of years to road test itself through evolution, would not go quietly – especially since it could sense victory in sight.

I began to speak and stumbled on my words. I looked at the audience, smiled nervously and continued, unfortunately at the wrong spot. I apologised, refocused on my notes, but by this time, fear had taken over my show. I pushed on, pretending that everything was OK which only exacerbated my increasingly embarrassing situation. My breathing became restricted, my voice was breaking up, my mouth went dry and my body language was indicating I was in free fall without a parachute. I just wanted some previously unknown sink hole below me to open and allow me to disappear. I think my audience, by now, had a similar wish.

My mind continued to race, caught between trying to refocus on presenting, whilst simultaneously having to put out a series of bush fires raging within. The fires were winning, and I was ready to surrender. I mumbled a few incoherent apologies and slunk off the stage, conscious of the awkward silence, which was shouting at me from my flummoxed audience.

I reached the safety of the stage's wings around about the same time my sense of deep public embarrassment began to descend on me. My first thoughts in response to this was to book a trip to South America and get a facelift. My second was that I would never open my mouth in public again. I was going to live the rest of my life as a strong, silent type – possibly a fisherman in the far North.

In the years following, I attempted to dissect that afternoon's experience and identify why I had been so derailed. There was no threat to my wellbeing in that room, beyond a potential paper cut from the flip charts. I knew that public speaking events could certainly cause nervousness. That was common knowledge, but I had zero appreciation of what a full-blown fight or flight take-down could feel like. I have experienced threatening situations before, though nothing comparable to that which military personnel or first responders such as firefighters or rescuers get to face. I have been through life and death events within my family, I have been shot, I have worked as a bouncer, I have trekked in Alaskan mountains with my son out in the open with three metre Kodiak bears, I have survived a massive storm at sea on a small yacht and my career in martial arts has thrown up many significant and varied tests over the four decades. Though I have felt fear in these experiences, I was never so incapacitated as I was on that podium and yet the potential 'danger' confronting me was imagined. Reflecting on this story, I draw solace from an observation by Jerry Seinfeld, who quipped on the subject of public speaking being the leading fear in the United States, even greater than death.

> 'Put it this way, most of us would prefer to be in the coffin than giving the eulogy!'

So *why* does the mind/body overreact to such situations as public speaking? *How* does fear do its thing? *What* can be done to mitigate such experiences? To explore the answers to these questions, we will draw from contemporary neuroscience as a starting point.

The chemistry of fear

Fear is an emotional response caused by a perceived threat which is either real or imagined. The fear could be related to the past, the future, or have its source in the immediate present. It can visit you with a gentle nudge, hit like a hand grenade or build up over time, like an ever-tightening vice. For many, fear is a daily companion, visiting in the forms of deeply embedded phobias. The response to experiencing fear can range from the slightest of increases in heart rate to a major emergency reaction where the entire resources of the mind/body are harnessed to confront a life-threatening situation.

The process which triggers a rapid response to fear is frequently 'sloppy' or poorly calibrated by the limbic system, which is otherwise known as the 'emotional brain'. The hyper speed at which a response is unleashed in the mind/body can result in a reaction that is either unwarranted or disproportionate. This happens because we have developed, through evolution, the capacity for quick fire, short cut responses to avoid injury or death. This is referred to as a neural *back alley*. The manager of this process is the amygdala, a small set of glands in the limbic part of the brain which controls the process to either fight, flight or freeze when a threat is perceived. *Fight* relates to an act of assertion or aggression; *flight* is where movement away from the threat is the default and *freeze* is associated with concealment in some form. This could refer to literally hiding, or in other cases, veiling your true thoughts and feelings behind a 'masked' expression. Though poorly calibrated at times, there is much to appreciate in this fight, flight or freeze process. The fact our species has survived, whilst many others are no longer around, is testimony to its effectiveness.

Having stated this, the system certainly could do with a software upgrade. When it comes to the immediate reaction to a threat – real, potential or imagined – the process travels through the same neural pathways and biochemical circuits that were within Trogg's brain, our distant cousin who existed over a million years ago. We have inherited this same process and it still suffers from a lack of finesse. It will trigger the same fight or flight response to a sneer from a work colleague as it would to being stalked by a tiger. Though the reaction to the tiger will be far greater, both responses will use the same wiring and release the same biochemistry.

It is easy to understand why meeting a tiger on your path or being on the receiving end of a road rage incident causes the survival instincts to kick in, but why a sneer? According to University of Alabama psychologist, Dolf Zillman, the universal trigger for anger is being endangered.[1] This is something of a no brainer; however, the contexts that 'being endangered' covers is where things get illuminating. A sense of endangerment can arise not just from an obvious physical threat, but also from;

> '...a symbolic threat to self-esteem or dignity, being insulted or demeaned, being frustrated in pursuing an important goal. These perceptions act as an instigating trigger for a limbic surge ... what we have been calling the fight or flight reaction.'[2]

So what?

The key point here relates to appreciating how the perception of endangerment, even if it is just associated with a sneer or a negative comment from another, can act to launch the survival process. To fully appreciate the implications of this process, and there are many, we need to broaden our understanding of how the brain works. This requires an exploration of the central nervous system. In this exploration, there is crucial information here to help you understand how and why the techniques outlined in later chapters do in fact work.

The Central Nervous System – A brief journey

The central nervous system (CNS) includes the brain and an important subsystem within it called the limbic system. The CNS is an extremely complex part of our internal engineering, incorporating both hardware and software. This chapter will provide a high-level glimpse into the multiple roles this system serves. The intent of this exploration is to build awareness regarding how the brain responds to threats. Implicit with this is the role that both fear and anger play in generating this process. With awareness of how these systems play out there comes an enhanced capacity to make conscious and constructive interventions when such powerful emotions arise. You will understand the why behind the shortness of breath, the racing of the heart, the dryness in the mouth and why it feels like your IQ has gone on a break and cave woman or man is running the show. The best place to start this exploration into our twenty first century brain is to take a quick trip through evolution.

According to most theories, our contemporary brain has evolved over millions of years. This process has been driven by the need to both survive and evolve in dangerous environments. Through this evolutionary journey the brain grew outwards in successive layers within the skull. The current twenty first century model reveals its ancestry with the most primitive feature, the brain stem, at the centre, and the most modern, the cerebrum, with its highly developed outer layer, the cortex, on the outside.[3] To give you some appreciation of just how well our brain has developed, please reflect on the following statistics.

The brain's hardware, made up of intricately arranged atoms and molecules, contains approximately 86 billion neurons and weighs in at one and a half kilos. Since every neuron can fire and inundate thousands of adjacent neurons with thousands of signals as many as 200 times per second, it is estimated that the brain can perform up to 38 million billion operations per second.[4]

Impressive! Pause for a moment and reflect on those incredible stats and the amazing piece of engineering mastery they belong to that drives our existence each day. With that much computing power available, it is surprising that we still make stupid mistakes. Of interest, Marco Magrini, the author of 'The Brain: A User's Manual', from which this quote was drawn, debunks the myth that we only use 10% of our brain. We will now move on to exploring the wider functioning of the brain as it expresses itself through the CNS.

Our entire nervous system comprises three main subunits: the Central Nervous System (CNS), the Peripheral Nervous System (PNS) and the one most relevant to our exploration, the Autonomic Nervous System (ANS). The CNS which contains the brain and spinal cord is responsible for the functioning of the entire nervous system. The PNS creates the links between the CNS and other body parts ranging from the head to the toes. The ANS controls and coordinates the body's automatic functions such as breathing, heart rate, digestion and excretion. Within the ANS there are two distinct subdivisions: the parasympathetic function and the sympathetic function. The parasympathetic function has more of a 'peacetime' role such as contributing to the effective process of digestion, lowering heart rate and blood pressure and regulating breathing rate. The sympathetic function is associated with preparing the body for action and to meet potential threats or to respond to excitement.[5] How the sympathetic nervous system functions is critical in understanding the way fear is experienced in the mind/body. This will be detailed shortly. At this point, continuing to give a high-level perspective, we will travel back to our evolutionary past, to explore the role of the limbic system.

The limbic system is a 'collective term for a group of interconnected brain structures that are involved in behaviours associated with survival including the expression of emotion, feeding, drinking, defence and reproduction as well as the formation of memory'.[6] This system evolved from the primitive brain stem and as it did, two powerful tools emerged, learning and memory, giving mammals a distinct evolutionary advantage over their less evolved contemporaries.[7] The capacity to consciously 'learn' and then remember this learning, was at the forefront of the success of mammals.

Also housed in the brainstem is the thalamus which acts as a central sensory relay station between the 'lower centres' of the brain and the hypothalamus. These two characters, the thalamus and the hypothalamus, play a central role in this guide. They function as communication hubs, sending and receiving signals between the higher, more evolved centres of the brain with the more primitive amygdala. They fulfil the crucial role of co-ordinating the initial response to a perceived threat and then the follow up investigation, assessing just how serious the threat is.

About a hundred million years ago the brain in mammals underwent another major evolutionary process with the emergence of another outer layer, the neocortex, which allowed for sophisticated mental processing which included thinking and awareness. The neocortex is the site where most cognitive functioning takes place. This includes subtle emotional responses such as 'having feelings about feelings' as its wiring is highly connected to the limbic system.[8] As well as these capabilities, the neocortex functions to discern the most suitable rational response to situations that arise in everyday life. When it comes to emotional emergencies however, such as a real or perceived threat, this highly capable and more recent enrolment in our brain evolution yields authority to the limbic system, in particular its much older go to action figure – the amygdala.

The amygdala

We have made passing reference already to the amygdala in context to the role it plays in orchestrating the fight, flight and freeze response. We will now do a deep dive into this process and explore how a perceived threat leads to an immediate sensation of fear which in turn, catalyses an amazing sequence of reactions in the mind/body.

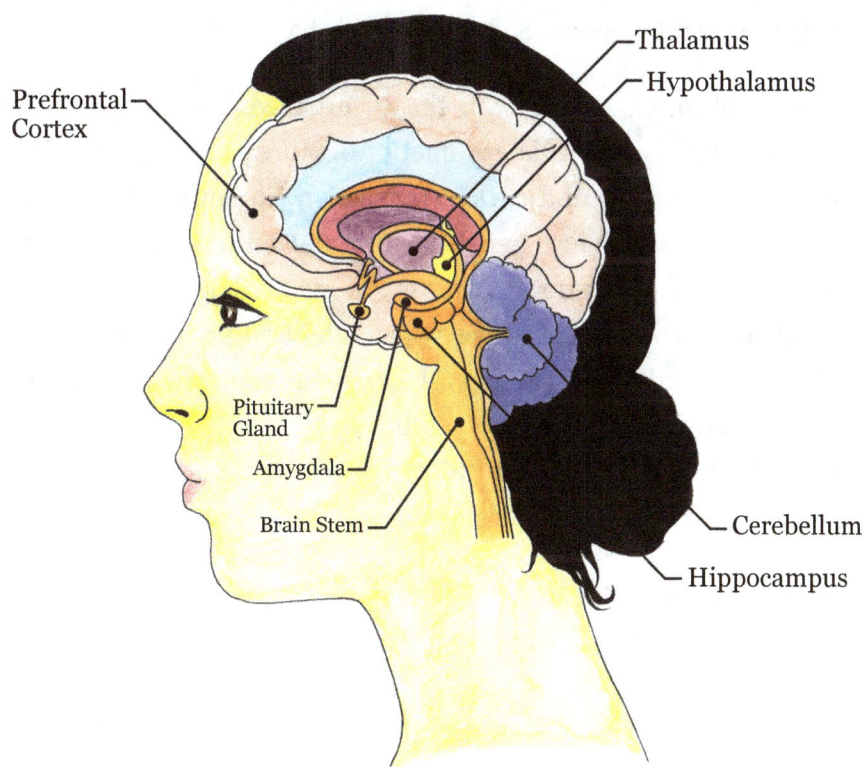

To illustrate this, we will use a story to track the biochemical and neural process which takes places during an amygdala hijack. This refers to the amygdala in full reactive mode, when it bypasses the more evolved (and slower) neocortex and temporarily takes charge. I have drawn from the wonderful book 'Blue Mind' by Wallace J Nicholls in shaping the content of this story.

When you swim in calm waters there is a good chance your mind/body is awash (pardon the pun) with feel good chemicals. If a sample of blood is taken at such times what would most likely show up is elevated levels of endorphins, oxytocin and dopamine all of which are activated during enjoyable physical activity such as swimming. If, however, while you're paddling among the waves, you notice a sudden and powerful disturbance of the surface water near you, this chemical cocktail will change at an exceptionally fast rate to facilitate a fight or flight reaction. So how does this happen?

The visual cortex, having 'seen' the disturbance, sends a signal to the limbic system for immediate evaluation of a threat. This happens faster than the conscious mind can kick into action. The answer flashed back is affirmative which acts to fire the amygdala into action. Your brain will be flooded with norepinephrine (which is known as the wake-up chemical) which helps focus your attention immediately on the place of disturbance. This is all happening almost instantaneously. The amygdala now readies your body for action by activating the sympathetic nervous system (SNS), preparing for a fight or flight as the disturbed water may conceal danger.

At this moment, you are charged with energy to fight or to flee. You are hypervigilant, staring at the place where the water was disturbed. In a few seconds your brain projects a series of potential matches for what caused the disturbance. A diving seabird, another swimmer, a seal, a dolphin and at the forefront – because we are wired to be risk averse – a shark. In response to this potential primary threat, and orchestrated by the amygdala, your hypothalamus signals to the adrenal glands to release adrenaline and norepinephrine, which act to boost the heart rate, sending blood surging to the large muscle groups as well as increasing oxygen uptake and processing in the lungs. This scrambling of your biochemistry to red alert levels is to enhance your capacity to confront a threat or to flee from it. A few seconds before, you were in la la land, enjoying the gentle waves. Now that feel good chemistry has been 'hijacked', as has your brain function, by the amygdala and its chemical dictates. Your inner peacenik has been shoved out of the picture by your chemical version of the SAS. Survival is the primary objective. To ensure there is no lapse in your highly alert state, cortisol continues to pour into your amygdala causing it to keep priming the SNS. You turn quickly towards the beach and swim with a speed commensurate with an Olympian, not pausing until your legs, which by now feel like jelly, are safely kicking up sand. Only then do you take a few deep breaths, turn around and see clearly for the first time a group of dolphins playing where you had just been swimming. As the adrenaline induced high heart rate begins to subside and your mind/body begins to adjust back to peacetime functioning, you reflect with some degree of amazement and respect, how little time, just a handful of seconds, it took from the first signal of danger to having your feet safely ensconced in sand.[9]

This scenario outlines how the amygdala, when activated in an emergency, runs a 'matching' process to identify the threat. In describing the role of the amygdala, Daniel Goleman uses a very effective analogy in his bestselling book, 'Emotional Intelligence'.

> *In the brain's architecture, the amygdala is poised something like an alarm company where operators are standing ready to*

send out emergency calls to the fire department, police and a neighbour whenever a home security system signals trouble.

It is a smaller, shorter pathway – something like a neural back alley – and allows the amygdala to receive some direct inputs from the senses and start a response before they are fully registered by the neocortex. The amygdala can have us spring into action while the slightly slower – but more fully informed – neocortex unfolds its more refined plan for reaction.

This 'spring' into action usually results in either: a fight response, where you literally 'step up' to confront a situation; flight, where you avoid or flee what is happening; or freeze, which can be associated with 'camouflaging' where you are present but remain quiet and most likely withdrawn.

The amygdala can house memories and response repertoires that we enact without quite realising why we do so because the shortcut from thalamus to amygdala completely bypasses the neocortex. This bypass seems to allow the amygdala to be the repository for emotional impressions and memories that we have never known about in full awareness. Its method of comparison is <u>associative</u>: when one key element of a present situation is similar to the past, it can call it a 'match'— which is why this circuit is sloppy: it acts before there is full confirmation.[10]

This 'matching' process is important in understanding why we often have a disproportionate reaction to a perceived threat or situation where we simply make a wrong call, with what can be dire consequences. In 2014 the former South African Rugby Union player Rudi Visagiea fired a shot at someone he thought was stealing his car. On hearing his car start in the early hours of the morning and having recently been the victim of a car theft, he fired out the bedroom window killing the driver. The 'thief' turned out to be his nineteen-year-old daughter. In terms of the amygdala process, a danger was perceived, a 'match' made and action taken very quickly. In extreme situations when an amygdala hijack occurs, it is important to realise that your ability to reason is impaired. This underscores the need to pause, when you are highly adrenalised and give your rational processes a chance to calibrate an appropriate reaction.

Tip

After an intense fight/flight experience, adrenaline and cortisol often stay in the body at elevated levels for hours and even days after, keeping you in varying degrees of readiness to meet or re-meet the *threat*. Therefore, after an experience of being highly adrenalised, you are more prone to being reactive, as you are still in a semi-prepared state for fight or flight. So, when the kids don't put their bikes away or your flatmate hasn't cleaned up, and your reaction is to put on a performance outdoing Russell Crowe in his final battle scene in Gladiator, you probably need to pause, reflect upon how 'wound up' you are and take a few deep breaths.

Keeping you alive

For the many times you have felt a victim of your amygdala's overreaction, or felt fear when you shouldn't, there have been countless times, mostly unconscious, that this function has been ensuring you have remained alive. The busy intersection, the rough surf, the decision to slow down the speed of your car, motorbike, boat, skis, skateboard or the sense of caution you felt around certain individuals, all have involved the amygdala. In times of real danger, it will have coordinated your entire mind/body system to respond effectively to threats in seconds and in some situations, sub-seconds.

The fact that you, at some point in your life, may have overreacted to a harmless stimulus and taken flight is, if anything, a testimony to the effectiveness of the amygdala at work. Consider how dangerous it would be navigating through our very complex world without an amygdala to protect us. This is reality for some people and their experiences have helped science greatly expand the understanding of how the amygdala functions.

People with damaged or improperly functioning amygdala fail to react to stimuli that would normally cause fear. In serious cases, there is the need for constant and close supervision for these individuals. A walk near a busy street could easily turn fatal.[11] Damage to the amygdala can also result in a behaviour called 'loss aversion'. This means those individuals who have this impairment may be prone to taking risks which outweigh, on a relative scale, the potential gains on offer.[12] This research undertaken by the California Institute of Technology highlights the important role the amygdala plays in helping calibrate returns relative to risk. This capacity to inject caution into everyday decision-making is a real value add and, as it happens, beneath the threshold of the conscious mind so amygdala fails to receive the appreciation that it deserves.

The hypothalamus

The other key players involved in the process of keeping us alive and deserving of a deeper exploration are the hypothalamus and the hippocampus. First the hypothalamus.

This fascinating entity is housed just above the brainstem. A snapshot of its job description follows.

> *By regulating hormone production in the pituitary gland and through the neural connections with other parts of the brain and spinal cord, the hypothalamus provides overall control of the autonomic nervous system which coordinates activity in the body's internal organs. It contains centres which regulate heart and blood pressure and plays a pivotal role in the expression of emotion such as fear, anger and pleasure.*[13]

As the amygdala 'perceives' a threat and sends out the signals to fight, flight or freeze, the hypothalamus, through its pivotal role in governing the ANS, functions as a relay station, transferring these signals forward to their points of execution. This brings into the picture the hippocampus.

The hippocampus

The role of this highly specialised entity lies in formulating memories. This is when newly acquired knowledge, where you have learnt or experienced something for the first time, is transferred to memory. As an example, our early ancestors may have discovered a new edible plant. Once the transference has taken place, this new information builds on what currently exists and then creates a new, expanded folio of knowledge to do with edible plants. According to Goleman, this process represents the heart of learning.[14] This is because we remember what we have learnt and can continually draw from and build upon this dynamic and evolving process.

In situations where there is heightened emotion such as fear, anger or excitement, the hippocampus will register these memories with greater detail. This is for a good reason. Under life-threatening situations, when the emotions are highly charged, there will be valuable survival lessons to acquire and pass on. In the future, if a similar threat occurs, there is a store of clearly filed information available in the hippocampus to help guide the response. This neural process is well appreciated by the military. When training recruits, part of the indoctrination is to expose them to live fire. Though the environment is controlled, it is still highly stressful and dangerous. This immersive experience is to help soldiers respond effectively when confronted with battle, for under real fire, they can draw on their stored memories of their training experiences. These memories are housed in the hippocampus.

Experiences in real warfare can also have a long and influential shelf life. My father was a World War II veteran who served in the Middle East and the Pacific. Long after hostilities ended, the sound of a backfiring car would cause him to instantaneously duck his head. The years of exposure to mortar fire during the war caused this involuntary reaction. In his case, the cause and effect neural connectivity was fused in the heat of real battle. Even though he was aware of this reaction he could not override it. The wiring went too deep.

Due to its critical role in memory formation and storage, the hippocampus has become a focus of extensive research, in particular to do with Alzheimer's disease.[15] When a hippocampus is damaged either through injury or degeneration, as it is in Alzheimer's, the usual effect is that older, longer term memories are still accessible; however the process of registering, storing and recalling newly formed knowledge, i.e. short term memories, is either impaired or not functioning at all. Exposure to prolonged periods of emotional distress can also impact the hippocampus. This effect is caused by elevated cortisol levels brought on by the stress. When stress is prolonged, cortisol levels build which in turn can affect the production of neurons in the hippocampus.

This may result in reduced numbers of neurons produced which can have very deleterious effects on learning.[16]

Educators face complex challenges in the light of this recent research. Moderate levels of cortisol do not negatively affect information uptake and can act to assist with memory retention. Therefore, how do you create a learning environment and structure a curriculum which is sensitive to the effects of stress? For what represents excessive stress for one student can be experienced as productive for another. The capacity for students to be able to self-regulate is critical in this context, so that when they are confronting excessive stress, they can take steps to mitigate this pressure. Mindfulness training, meditation and exercise are among the most useful interventions in this case. These skills will be detailed in the coming chapters.

An important learning from the animal kingdom

Humans have a tendency to believe that the internal software developed along our evolutionary path is superior to other mammals. When it comes to survival engineering, the facts tell a different story. We suffer from some significant glitches compared to our four-legged friends.

Picture a zebra grazing at peace on the African plains. Some disturbing scent causes her to cease feeding. She lifts her head and on the edge of her peripheral vision the silhouette of a stalking lioness is picked up. Her sympathetic nervous system takes over instantaneously causing adrenal glands to fill her body with a great charge of energy. She is rapidly propelled to top speed, outpacing the lioness and eventually after a short sprint she feels safe enough to slow down and eventually begins to graze again. Her internal homeostasis will shortly resume. So why could this be considered a 'superior' system than ours? We have a very similar fight or flight system in place, as outlined. Unlike animals, the difference with humans is that we can turn on our fight or flight response by thought alone.[17] This happens regardless of how relevant this response is at the time it is triggered. The amygdala can be switched on by a sense of anticipation of something which is encroaching – a job interview, a difficult conversation, a date – or something that could happen. This switch can also be activated by trawling in memory banks, causing sad and painful experiences to resurface.

In the context of firing up our fight/flight process, we can learn from the zebra. Enjoy the surroundings, live in the moment, hang out with your friends and if genuine danger threatens, act quickly. And finally, be cautious of allowing your thoughts to dwell too much on the past, as it may not be helpful and in doing so, you will miss out on the richness of the present moment.

🛠 Toolbox: A simple question

The dictum – Energy flows where attention goes – is applicable here. A useful question to ask at any point in time is: *What am I thinking about now and is this helpful?*

We are often unconscious of when we have had a fight or flight response activated. Research in the United States using fMRI scanners identified that people exposed to photos of faces depicting a variety of emotions, including fear and anger, were not aware when their amygdala had been triggered.[18] The scanner however was able to clearly pinpoint the moments when the amygdala was activated, though the person being scanned had no conscious or physical awareness that this reaction was taking place. The implications of this research highlight a need to be cautious, when exposed to a fearful situation or environment, even when the threat is minimal or as in this case, below our conscious threshold. Our system is still registering and responding which entails energy expenditure. This is like having the light on in the glove compartment of a car and being unaware of it. Over time the battery gets drained. Applying this analogy to life, if you feel yourself exposed to a low gradient of fear over a prolonged period of time – a workplace which is really toxic for example – a change of environment may be a wise move for your health.

In this chapter, we have defined fear, outlined how it is generated, met some of the main characters in this process – the amygdala, the neocortex, the hypothalamus and the hippocampus – and given honourable mentions to adrenaline and cortisol. With this information in place, the focus will shift to exploring the upside of our survival engineering and learn how to use it constructively and avoid becoming a victim to it.

Chapter 3: Rewiring your 'firing' – the 'how to' of changing behaviours

Neuroplasticity

For centuries, the scientific view regarding brain functionality was that we are born with a certain amount of grey matter and over a lifetime of use and misuse, this supply continues to dwindle and dwindle until death finally claims us. Research over the last couple of decades clearly indicates this is not the case. New scientific insights demonstrate how the brain has an implicit capacity to grow itself by forming new neural pathways. The agency which enables this is called neuroplasticity, defined by neuroscientist Christopher Bergland as:

> *'the ability of the brain to form new connections and pathways and change how its circuits are wired.'* [1]

Supporting this remarkable process is another called neurogenesis. This refers to the brain's ability to grow new neurons.

One could speculate that this process (neuroplasticity and neurogenesis) opens up the possibility to reinvent yourself and move away from the status quo or to overcome past traumatic events that evoke anxiety and stress. Hardwired fear-based memories often lead to avoidant behaviours that can hold you back from living your life to the fullest.[2]

This statement has profound implications. If you are desiring a reset in your life, your brain is highly capable of facilitating the process. This provides real hope for individuals wishing to create constructive changes in their life. The process lies in rewiring our thinking, which in turn can change the way we behave. So how does it work? Your brain is constantly engaged and active, including during all stages of sleep. It never really rests, just registers differing levels of output. Where there is consistent attention, for example learning a new skill such as a musical instrument, or language, the parts of the brain which facilitate this will develop a greater density of circuitry. Below is a shorthand summary of this process by Dr David Rock drawn from his book, 'Your Brain at Work'.[3]

- The brain is a collection of neural pathways which are the result of neurons firing and connecting.

- Every time we are faced with a stimulus, the neurons fire and connect, thereby strengthening and reinforcing the neural pathways for that specific stimulus.

- Whatever we give consistent long-term attention and focus to becomes the neural pathway equivalent of a six-lane highway.

- When focussing on something new the initial connection is like a goat track – if we don't reinforce it, this connection will always be weak or even disappear.

Putting this in another way, using the words of Canadian scientist Donald Hebb;

> *'Neurons that fire together wire together. This means that neurons that fire together connect and reinforce their reciprocal links. By creating new synapses, reinforcing old ones and cutting away those that are no longer needed, the brain constantly re-organises the relations between its neurons.'*[4]

The critical point in these scientific snapshots is that if you really desire to transform a certain behaviour or dysfunctional pattern, you need to discipline where your attention goes. Without thinking new thoughts and believing in new possibilities, your existing patterns will continue to act as a default. This in turn continues to reinforce the wiring and firing along existing neural pathways. This default reflects the *passive* approach. The newer, exploratory 'goat tracks' that you may have created will get quickly diminish into irrelevance if they are not given regular focus. As an alternative, in taking an *active* approach, you can consciously change your life by redirecting where your thinking and attention is focused. Due to neuroplasticity, if the new modes of thinking, i.e. 'goat tracks', are given sustained attention, these newly imprinted thought lines can be turned into favoured pathways. A simple example of this is learning an instrument. If you are passionate about what you are doing and practise regularly, the continuous improvement is evident. The muscle memory is created and your playing moves more from a conscious process, where you are focused on reading the notes, to more of an unconscious, flow experience. If this works in the process of learning an instrument, what about the process of learning to view yourself, or the life you live, through a different lens? If fear in some form is acting to limit you, can you start to change your habitual thinking patterns as a catalyst to reset your behaviours? In being disciplined with what you think and where your attention is drawn to, you may discover the fear you have been dealing with has no substance beyond the power you have given it.

There is the potential for widespread utilisation of the principles underpinning neuroplasticity in the education system. As a former teacher, I found dealing with students with low self-esteem, little confidence and plagued by insecurities a relatively common experience. In observing this dynamic at close hand, it was clear to see a damaging pattern at play. Negative thoughts acting to generate negative feelings, which in turn fuelled self-destructive behaviours. In understanding how wiring is established in the brain, i.e. through neuroplasticity, it is easier to understand how these negative patterns of thinking become re-enforcing loops.

The axiom *'what gets fired, gets wired'* points to a way to help break these negative patterns of thinking and shift them to more constructive ones. Whatever the context, the process of self-healing must begin with the individual being willing to question old patterns and think in new and different ways. This can happen when someone who is afflicted with some form of depression or anxiety can begin to envisage a future which is better than the 'state' they are currently in. Also, it occurs when overly negative and destructive cycles of thinking and behaving are shifted towards a more self-affirming and self-loving way of being in the world. What can contribute to this reset in thinking is the introduction of a simple tool which acts to intervene between a stimulus and how you think about and ultimately respond to this stimulus. This tool we will call the 'pause button' and it is explored in depth in the next chapter.

So what?

The key point in this chapter is the need for vigilance; be aware of what draws your attention, as specific parts of the brain will be activated and develop according to the frequent focus. *What gets fired, gets wired!* If you do wish to experience more flow in your life, it could it be as simple as reviewing where your attention gets snagged, where fear is given too much unwarranted oxygen and where you have been either too lazy, too invested, or too comfortable to re-evaluate and reset your thinking and behavioural patterns.

Chapter 4:
The humble (though highly valuable) pause button

Between stimulus and response there is a space. In that space is our power to choose our response.

Viktor Frankl

There have been times in my life where I wish I could have been able to impose some form of a remote control over my life. *Rewinding* when I recognised that I made poor decisions and hitting the fast forward when I experienced boredom or had been floundering. Though these are just musings of the mind there is one function available – the *pause*.

🧰 Toolbox: The pause button

The pause button is a wonderful tool, with wide application for a complex and challenging world. The above diagram, inspired by the work of Stephen Covey, captures this concept. A stimulus (S) occurs. This could arrive in the form of an argument, an opportunity, an idea, a threatening look, a challenging conversation or a request

for help landing in your inbox. Before you act, the key idea is hit the metaphorical 'pause button' and weigh your options prior to responding (R). This is a clear example of taking an active position for you are consciously making decisions regarding what is before you. When you fail to pause, or you take a passive position, the tendency is to default to a well-worn pattern of response that you have developed previously when you have faced similar stimuli.

As an example, reflect on your ability to either say no and/or set boundaries. If you are forever saying yes when an honest and considered response would be *no*, you are demonstrating a passive default pattern. Remember what you consistently *fire* gets *wired*. In situations like this, hitting the pause button and making a clear, conscious choice, followed by an affirmative action, can really help break a limiting pattern. This is the pause button acting as a circuit breaker. You stop long enough to make a considered response instead of enacting a rushed reaction. And if diligently applied overtime, this little button can literally change lives. How does this happen? The willingness to pause in order to make a conscious decision is a hallmark of someone who feels personally empowered and confident. They do not go into automatic passive mode when a decision is required and because of this there is opportunity for continuous growth and learning. The downside of defaulting to a *passive* response is well illustrated in this popular saying;

> *'Always do what you have always done and you will always get what you have always got!'*

Case Study

When you are confronted by a situation which is genuinely dangerous, the amygdala's call to either combat stations (fight) or to leap onto the fastest horse (flight) may represent the best choices. However, in situations where there is no real threat to your wellbeing, responding to your amygdala's impelling directives can have unfortunate consequences. I am sure Zinedine Zidane, the French soccer star, would concur with this observation. At the 2006 World Cup he could have been well served by utilising a pause button. The French star was the target of repeated and very intentional niggling by his Italian opponent Materazzi. His 'thoughtful' response came in the manner of a head butt, flattening the Italian defender in front of the referee, match audience and hundreds of millions of viewers. This resulted in his immediate send-off and arguably the reason why the French, now without their key player, lost that critical game. Whether you are into sport or not, I am sure you can recognise that this was a classic example of the amygdala hijack in action; an overreaction in this case, which could have been avoided if Zidane had taken a pause instead of retaliating. He could have considered his options and then replied something as simple as *"Thank you for sharing with me your observations on my family members Mr Materazzi."* Who knows, France may have had another World Cup to add to their collection.

Using the Zidane example, if you track the news cycle in any given week, you will hear similar stories, which in one way or another, refer to a disproportionate reaction someone has taken to something that has happened to them. These stories emanate from the sporting fields, the law courts, from war zones and even disgruntled neighbours and frequently detail excessive and unwarranted use of violence. In their defence, the perpetrator often refers to a moment of uncontrolled madness, when they 'lost it' or had a 'brain snap', experienced a 'meltdown', or saw the 'red mist'. These descriptions refer to the amygdala hijack explained in Chapter 2. Will Smith's slap on the face of Chris Rock during the 2022 Oscars is a classic, and like Zidane, very public example of an amygdala hijack. The application of a 'pause' could certainly help in such situations. This would be a 'pause' just long enough to draw in a few breaths, take stock and choose a constructive response. Otherwise, one's life can take a drastic and destructive turn, pivoting on a simple, unwise decision to allow cave man or woman to momentarily be in control.

The great quality of the pause button is that it can be used and re-used continually. It never wears out, costs nothing and is always demonstrating an adaptive and agile set of uses. Years back a good friend of mine spoke to me about how he and his eighteen-year-old son were having some significant challenges, which included very heated exchanges. Both were large alpha style personalities, giving truth to the old adage – *the apple not falling far from the tree.* In such dynamics, when people are being combative with one another, the amygdala switches into full fight mode, causing the momentarily 'irrelevant' rational mind to take a back seat. Using his words, the strategy he landed upon was to "strike when the iron is ... cold". When things were shaping up towards a potential clash, he would suggest a later time for the conversation and then take himself off for a walk, to cool the iron. This represents a simple, effective strategy – the use of a 'pause'. He was not avoiding a difficult conversation or situation, but just suspending it till there were fewer caveman hormones present and a better chance of achieving a mutually beneficial outcome.

This ability to make conscious choices regarding how you respond to people and situations is an example of the interplay between self-awareness and self-regulation. Being self-aware, you have cognition of how you are interpreting what is happening around you and within you.

Self-regulation refers to employing choice, frequently demonstrated as restraint, in how you respond to the events of everyday life.

> *Our emotions are driven by biological impulses. These biological impulses are beyond our control, but the resulting emotions are not. When emotions are high, they certainly cannot be ignored – but they can be carefully managed. This is called self-regulation and it's the quality of emotional intelligence that liberates us from living like hostages to our impulses.*[1]

According to Daniel Goleman, who has published extensively on the subject, a person who knows how to self-regulate possesses:

- An inclination towards reflection and thoughtfulness
- Acceptance of uncertainty and change
- Integrity – specifically the ability to say no to impulsive urges.[2]

The ability to self-regulate is a great competency to have and one that can be easily developed.

Tip 1

When your amygdala has been triggered – something has been said, a scowl or some cynical comment has been expressed towards you – and you are about to respond with indignation, return fire, plot for a later revenge or flee, instead of these options, remember the pause button. Simply take a breath, create a space before you react so you can assess your options and then consciously choose your response. Regularly using the pause button in one's life is guaranteed to save you friendships, prevent you from making CLMs (career limiting moves) and assist in you sleeping well because you have not been kept up all night regretting what you had said or done that day in the heat of the moment.

Tip 2

When taking a 'pause' you do not have to respond immediately. It can be in the next hour, the next day or next week. Ignore the need to feel compelled to respond in the moment. A simple response could be... "That's a very interesting proposition. Let me think about it and I will get back to you tomorrow". Give yourself breathing space and time to assess what your options are.

So what?

Practising hitting the pause button, being able to stop, reflect and consciously choose a response, certainly enhances the capacity to create calm in the mind and manage fear. Putting it simply, this refers to your ability to reset in the moment and reclaim being present.

The 'pause' helps create the capacity to discern: what is worthy of a response; what can be ignored or shelved; and if a response is required, what shape it may take and how it will be delivered. There are many forms in which your pause button may manifest; the draft box on your email, a quick break for a water or coffee, a comment assuring the other that you will respond in time, or just simply a deep in-breath, followed by a moment to reflect.

The genesis of this idea of the pause came out of an unlikely source, the Holocaust. The concept, popularised by the American writer Stephen Covey, has its origins in the work of Viktor Frankl. Frankl was an Austrian psychiatrist who survived Auschwitz and numerous other concentration camps during World War II. After surviving the war, he published 'Man's Search for Meaning' which details his personal experience of the death camps. The book is remarkable for its understated quality given the horrors upon which it is based. What builds to become a central theme is Frankl's growing realisation that regardless of what was happening to him; beatings, incredible deprivation of rights, near starvation and the ever-present potential of his own death, his captors ultimately could not determine his response to what was happening to him. This was for his choosing.

> *'We who lived in concentration camps can remember the men who walked through the huts comforting others, giving away their last piece of bread. They may have been few in number, but they offer sufficient proof that everything can be taken away from a man but one thing: the last of the human freedoms – to choose one's attitude in any given set of circumstances, to choose one's own way.'* [3]

The book offers readers an opportunity to reflect on what is really important in life and what amounts to genuine hardship. It is worth considering the amount of energy and time wasted by being frustrated when confronting such trivial inconveniences as traffic jams, office skirmishes and poor service. Frankl faced the very real potential of his own death, every day for four years and yet during this horrific period, he still managed to maintain his attention on what he believed to be truly important, inspiring and meaningful in life. Of these qualities, one instinct remained constant, the need to help others. He carried out this personal mission with as much effort and dignity as he could muster, despite his ever-weakening health and the constant exposure he faced to a multitude of threats. When he was finally released at the war's end and could assess the totality of what he had endured, he came away, paradoxically, with an enriched view of the human condition.

Frankl observed that those who managed to survive in the camps were usually driven by a sense of purpose, a why! This is reflected in his statement;

'Those who have a 'why' to live, can bear with almost any 'how'.'[4]

His why was motivated by two compelling drives; a search for meaning, made all the more significant by the horrors that surrounded him and a more personal, cherished hope to be reunited with his wife and family after the war. This hope was not to be fulfilled, as his wife, along with his father and brother, all perished in the death camps.

His search for meaning however did continue, decades after the war and helped inspire the creation of his personal brand of psychotherapy known as logotherapy. At the core of this therapy lies the premise that the primary motivational force of an individual is to find meaning in life. Aligned with and supporting this central theme, he champions the importance of 'personal determinism'. This philosophy has at its core the belief that we can 'choose' our attitude to what we are experiencing, even in the most challenging of situations. His life was a demonstration of this capacity and one that we all can espouse. To enact this, we just need to create a pause between when something happens to us and how we *choose* to respond. And this brings us back to where we began this chapter – the 'pause button'. In Frankl's words;

'Between stimulus and response there is a space. In that space is our power to choose our response. In our response lies our growth and our freedom.'[5]

That space is where the pause button rests.

So, when fear next pays you a visit and you sense your amygdala kicking in and defaulting to a well-worn fight, flight or freeze reaction, use it as an opportunity for personal growth. Allow a space between the recognition of the fear and how you react, by hitting a metaphorical pause button and consciously choosing a considered and constructive response. This simple step could literally transform your life or at least some aspects of it.

Chapter 5: Fears, beliefs and behaviours.

Until you make the unconscious conscious, it will direct your life and you will call it fate.

Carl Jung

Now let's get personal and explore your unique collection of beliefs and behaviours associated with fear. In this chapter, you will be presented with a set of exercises designed to assist you to get clear as to the specific fear(s) you hold, the beliefs that accompany these fears and the behaviours that result from these beliefs. We are now moving from the theory to the practical.

Naming fears

This exercise begins with the simple, yet profound activity of identifying the fear or fears you wish to work with. This action, mundane as it may seem, is a critical first step. When you can name a specific fear, understand where it has originated and recognise the behaviours that it generates, you are on the path towards embracing it and having a more constructive relationship with it. This process of 'naming' fears and other elements within your psyche is reflected in the renowned fantasy novel, 'A Wizard of Earthsea'.

A Mage (magician) can control only what is near him, what he can name exactly and wholly.[1]

Written by Ursula K Le Guin, this story is rich with wisdom, insight and meaning. It follows the heroic adventures of a young apprentice, known as Ged, who is on a journey to become a fully-fledged wizard. The story turns around a fateful moment, when Ged, attempting to show off, accidently chants an incantation incorrectly and in doing so, releases a 'darkness' that emerges from the 'fabric' of the universe. The presence of this entity fills him with dread and impels him to flee in fear of his life. Through numerous adventures he begins to understand, the more he runs from this 'darkness' the greater its strength becomes. In the final moments, with the darkness descending upon him, with nowhere to escape, he has a timely epiphany. He realises that this darkness is his shadow, that part of him which he has denied and suppressed, and the more he runs from it and denies it as being part of himself, the more he feeds it strength. He resolves the situation by turning to face the darkness and claiming it as part of himself. He names it. In doing so, he rids himself of the shadow's influence.

The author is a Jungian by training and this influence is clearly present in her writings. Jung was fascinated by the manner the unconscious influences our daily lives, especially those elements which are either denied, unidentified or suppressed. These elements are described as being unintegrated and existing in one's shadow, as demonstrated by the fear in Ged's shadow. To integrate these elements, such as fear, anger, shame, jealousy and guilt, into conscious awareness requires clarity about their true nature. This refers to what these emotions represent; how, why and when they show up, the impact they bring, and the implications this has on your life. With conscious awareness, i.e., by naming them, an individual can begin to have a more healthy and conscious relationship with them. They can be brought into the light and removed from 'the shadow' dimensions of the psyche. In doing so, their capacity to cause disruption and pain is reduced.

This next exercise is intended to achieve something similar, to shine a light on your shadow, in particular where your fears live. In doing this, we start the practical process towards embracing fear and finding flow!

> *A good place to start explaining the 'shadow' is with Jung himself.
>
> *'Unfortunately, there is no doubt about the fact that man is, as a whole, less good than he imagines himself or wants to be. Everyone carries a shadow and the less it is embodied (integrated) in the individual's conscious life, the blacker and denser it is. If an inferiority is conscious one always has a chance to correct it. Furthermore, it is constantly in contact with other interests, so that it is steadily subject to modifications. But if it is repressed and isolated from consciousness, it never gets corrected. It is, moreover, liable to burst forth in a moment of unawareness.'*
>
> Modern interpreters of Jung have also described the shadow as a sub-world of the psyche where the most primitive part of oneself is stored. This includes selfishness, repressed instinct and the 'unauthorised' self that your conscious mind rejects.[2]

Exercise: Identifying fears

The following exercise leads through a series of steps to identify what it is that you fear. The simple outcome is to be able to put a name to the fear(s). There are specific outcomes intended with this exercise: firstly, to increase self-awareness so that you are less likely to be taken by surprise, inhibited or worse still derailed when fear visits; secondly to build your muscle regarding options when dealing with fear; finally, to ask the question ... *Are there some fears that you no longer need to be paying attention to?* In some circumstances you may be simply replaying old patterns which are no longer relevant or warranted.

If you are not concerned by a specific fear or fears, you could skip this set of exercises and reconnect with the next chapter on Consciousness. Alternatively, if you are aware that you have numerous fears that you wish to work with, try just concentrating on one or two to help avoid any sense of overwhelm.

N.B. There is no claim here that this exercise can resolve long and deeply held fears. However, it may contribute to the journey towards resolving them, or at least minimising their impact. If in the process of working with this exercise strong emotions surface, please consider seeking professional help.

On the next page is a list of common fears. Tick all that apply. If your specific fear(s) is not listed, please add.

List of fears

Fear of ...

Being judged ☐	Success ☐
Failure ☐	Reaching your upper limit ☐
Loss of power/prestige/position ☐	Being different ☐
Loss of love ☐	Rejection ☐
Being loved ☐	Disapproval ☐
Change ☐	Loneliness ☐
Being vulnerable ☐	The unknown ☐
Being disliked ☐	Ridicule ☐
Being ineffective ☐	Being poor ☐
Confrontation ☐	Being alone ☐
Death ☐	Loss of freedom ☐
Being hurt ☐	Uncertainty ☐
Injury ☐	Being excluded ☐
Being ignored, not noticed ☐	Being discriminated against ☐
Being controlled ☐	Being treated unfairly ☐
Being trapped/confined/restricted ☐	Loss of health, well being ☐

Other:

It may seem strange that included in this list, are fears such as being loved and being successful. The reason behind their inclusion is simple. I have met people with these fears and when the reasons are explored in depth, the usual cause of the fear is associated with the 'disruption' which could happen. Their preference is to stay with the current status quo, a life they know which is predictable and controlled. Love and success can change all that and take people out of what they know to be their comfort zone. Also, it may require them to lose some form of control in their current ordered life.

Some more of the pathological fears:

Social phobias ☐	Generalised Anxiety Disorder ☐
Claustrophobia ☐	Obsessive Compulsive Disorder ☐
Agoraphobia ☐	Fear of heights ☐

Other:

Some specific fears in the world of business:

Making a CLM – career limiting move ☐	Being unfairly treated ☐
Giving feedback ☐	Loss of autonomy ☐
Receiving feedback ☐	Uncertainty ☐
Being judged/viewed as incompetent ☐	Loss of status and prestige ☐
Challenging superiors ☐	Loss of position ☐
Challenging group thinking ☐	Lack of promotion ☐
Being different ☐	Promotion ☐
Isolation ☐	Getting it wrong ☐
Technology ☐	Overload ☐
Ageism – Fear of being perceived too old/young for certain positions ☐	Feeling out of depth ☐
	Failing to deliver ☐
	Other:

Exercise: Unpacking this fear

Building on the preceding exercise, our focus will now shift to explore the origins of the fears you have identified. The second part of the exercise seeks to clarify the beliefs you have which are driven by these fears.

From the *List of fears*, identify the three most significant you want to work with. Put the most impactful at #1.

1. _____
   _____

2. _____
   _____

3. _____
   _____

Of these three fears, which one do you wish to first explore and in what situation or context? For example, Fear: Confrontation. Situation: At work.

Which fear: _____
_____

What situation: _____
_____

To use 'confrontation' as an example, you may have had some very challenging experiences in your childhood years at home, school or elsewhere that are clearly associated with the experience of 'confrontation'.

On a personal front, in the home I grew up in, confrontation was expressed through all gradients of anger, ranging from sarcasm to full-on aggression and ultimately violence. Nothing good came from it, as it was just a continual cycle of rehashing the same accusations and threats, the same heated arguments over the same issues on and on. Had some tangible benefit emerged from all the aggression, I may have developed a different, more positive view of anger. As it was, it took decades to review my perception of this emotion and come to an understanding that there is also a beneficial side to anger. Anger can be highly constructive if used appropriately. Such as when it is expressed in a respectful manner and with positive intent. It can be a highly effective agent of change.

The absence of conflict is not harmony, it is apathy.

K.M. Eisenhardt

Exercise: Towards letting go

Find a quiet place and some unhurried time and in the space below, write down everything you can remember about your history with the specific fear you have identified. Tip: don't censor your mind.

_____

_____

_____

_____

_____

_____

_____

_____

_____

_____

_____

_____

_____

_____

_____

_____

Reflection

When you reflect on these experiences, what beliefs about yourself and beliefs about this fear have you adopted? For example, with confrontation it may be – it is frightening, I am not good at it, nothing beneficial results from it, people always get hurt, etc.

List two key beliefs associated with the specific fear you have identified.

1. _____

   _____

2. _____
_____

Now reflect upon the following questions regarding the beliefs you have just listed.

Q: Do these beliefs still serve you in any meaningful way?
_____
_____

Q: Do they add value to your life?
_____
_____

Q: Has there been a payoff for holding this belief in the past?
_____
_____

Q: Are these beliefs still relevant to your life now?
_____
_____

Q: If they still serve you in some manner, are you willing to give them less airtime or prominence?
_____
_____

Q: Can you reframe or recast these beliefs? To give an example – a fear of confrontation could be reframed as; *Confrontation, done well, can be constructive and help move things forward when they are stuck.*
_____
_____

Q: Can you let go of these beliefs, because your life has moved beyond their use-by date?

_____

_____

This exercise is about building awareness. With an expanded field of awareness comes an increase in options. You will be in a better position to make conscious decisions when you feel powerful emotions surface such as fear or anger.

Reflection

I strongly suggest you spend some time reflecting here and not just pass over the exercise quickly. This is not intended to represent some personal fault-finding process but more to help understand what has contributed to your current mental models and motivations, specifically around fear. As you reflect on your notes;

Q: What actions could you take to let go of these outdated mental models?

_____

_____

Q: What new *firing* and *wiring* could you choose to focus on as you move forward with your life? As an example, if you have an overactive and vindictive inner critic, can you apply a diet for this entity? Conversely, can you direct more nourishment and airtime to your inner cheer squad?

_____

_____

Q: If there is still a lot of energy locked up in the past, particularly pain, do you need some professional help to sort through this?

_____

_____

So what?

Significant dynamics can play out in your life that have a root cause in fear. For example, difficulties in being committed in a relationship, avoiding conflict, playing less than, needing always to be in control, excessive need for approval and assurance from others, self-destructive behaviours and addictions to label a few common afflictions or 'issues'.

It can be helpful to identify the source from where specific fears may have emerged. I proffer *may* here, because caution is required in the process of discerning the sources of strong emotions. Some sources are indisputable such as exchanges with the class bully, whilst the cause of others may remain a mystery. In my primary school days, there were two brothers who were significantly larger than the rest of us and both possessed forearms like Popeye. Qualities such as empathy, compassion and gentleness missed their gene pool completely. Running from these gangsters, playing dead or voting to being one of their subservient Direct Reports proved to be smart moves. We got to play another day.

The point of this story is the next time you feel fear associated with a strong emotion, such as 'confrontation' in my case, realise there is a history to it. When a specific fear visits, the file is opened in the limbic system and the likely default is to a previously used, now outdated, coping mechanism. For example, running from or avoiding conflict, which you may have learnt to do in your school days, will no longer be the best option for you in your adult life.

Tip

What may be helpful to consider is not so much what has happened to you in the past, but how you now choose to interpret the experience. Was the experience really all that 'bad' and 'frightening' or did it just seem so at the time? Obviously, there are some decidedly terrifying experiences that people have endured, so this is not to discount the impact of such trauma. Instead, it is an opportunity to evaluate how much experience from the past still influences your current life and what options you have in relationship to this dynamic. Can you let go of these thoughts, stop revisiting them, or more simply view it through a different lens? Can you reframe them?

Chapter 6:
The dance of consciousness

All 'graduations' in human development mean the abandonment of a familiar position ... all growth ... must come to terms with this fact.

Erik H. Erikson

In this chapter, we will continue this theme of working with fears, beliefs and behaviours and go a touch deeper, exploring the interplay between the conscious and unconscious mind. Our starting point for this deep dive will be a model featuring an iceberg as its centre.

Concept: The iceberg analogy

Sigmund Freud, the acclaimed Austrian psychoanalyst, was the first to refer to an iceberg as being analogous to the conscious and unconscious mind. Although only the tip is visible on the surface of an iceberg, below the waterline there exists a much greater mass which is mostly unseen, unknown and unmapped. The shape and distribution of the weight of this mass affects what is seen on the surface. These qualities mirror Freud's perception of how the mind works, in particular the interplay between that which is visible (conscious mind) – actions, decisions, behaviours – with that which is invisible (unconscious mind).

> *Consciousness is the most difficult thing in the world because we don't know what it is. What's worse, we can't even define it. It's the ability to perceive and experiment. It's subjectivity. It's the awareness of oneself and one's environment. It's thought. It's free will. It's the control panel of the mind. It's all that and much more.*[1]

This diagram is a version of the now ubiquitous 'iceberg' analogy. Like the water which laps an edge of an iceberg, there is no real clear and constant demarcation line between the conscious and unconscious. They are both informing, influencing and shaping each other constantly. Self-awareness is essentially dropping this waterline, so that you become more aware, or conscious of, what you hold below this threshold. Beneath this waterline are your needs, your past experiences, beliefs based on these experiences, your values, your shadow, plus a whole world of feelings and thoughts. Becoming more conscious of this area enables greater choice.

If you desire to make sustainable change in your life, having some level of cognisance of the deeper drivers which inhabit your unconscious is a good place to start. The adjective 'sustainable' is selected because it suggests something which lasts. Short term change is easy such as weight loss, New Years' Resolutions, fitness fads and the like. I have a friend who gives up smoking weekly. Genuine and lasting transformation can be difficult due to the influence that beliefs, which have been built up and reinforced over time, hold in your conscious and unconscious mind. They are the 'roots' of the issue and for greater clarity, need to be understood and worked with. Due to the density of the wiring, that is the neural circuitry involved, short term attention will not bring about a sustainable transformation in behaviour. A longer term, dedicated approach is required. The place to start however is first to identify what

you wish to change and then create some new patterns of thinking and behaving. Complicating the process of moving away from unhealthy habits is the biochemistry connected with addictive behaviours. Excessive use of drugs (illegal as well as prescriptive), cigarettes and alcohol all cause changes in our biochemical makeup and neural wiring which makes moving on from an unhealthy habit more problematic. The place to start is with our thinking, using it as a key lever to change behaviour. A first step in this process could be to adopt the simple belief that you *can* create a better future.

Exercise: *Your personal iceberg*

In the previous chapter, we spent some time identifying fears and the beliefs associated with them. This next set of exercises deal with the negative or constraining behaviours which are generated by these fears as well as outlining some suggestions for moving beyond them.

Spend time to reflect on your own personal 'iceberg'. Above the surface and visible to the world are the actions you take and the behaviours you exhibit. Are there behaviours you wish to change? Some examples could be running or hiding from conflict, avoiding or sabotaging relationships, continuous self-criticism, always having to be in control, approval seeking or holding yourself back from opportunities, lacking confidence, arrogance, etc.

Q: Name the behaviour.
_____
_____

Q: How would you like to change and what would this look like?
_____
_____

Q: What would be the upside of transforming this behaviour to one which is more constructive?

_____
_____

Q: What are some pivotal steps you need to take? What is the first one?

_____
_____

Q: What may get in your way and if this shows up, how can you respond?

_____
_____

Q: In terms of transforming this behaviour, what will success look and feel like?

_____
_____

Over time, as you implement these changes and move away from destructive behaviours to those which are constructive, make sure you celebrate your successes along the way. This does not need to be dramatic. It can simply be a quiet moment to reflect on your progress and offer your good self an affirmative thought. Or it could come in the form of a small reward.

War stories

Two brief stories follow that illustrate the interplay between the conscious and unconscious mind. They deal with calamitous events which happened to two children, one English and the other Japanese, during World War II. The point of these stories is to illustrate how powerful experiences have the capacity to deeply sear the subconscious and continue to exert influence decades later. This often happens because traumatic events tend to generate protective beliefs and behaviours as a way to help avoid a re-experience of the trauma.

I once had the pleasure of working with an English lady, who as a young girl was living in Singapore when the Japanese troops overran the city in the opening stages of the Pacific War. In panic, her mother pushed her into a cupboard for safety, telling her if she made a noise, she and the rest of the family would be discovered and killed. That proved to be a turning point in her life. In the decades that followed she had great trouble in expressing herself through her voice and when she did, it was always with an extremely quiet and very polite delivery. I remember having to lean forward just to hear her. What was intriguing in this story was though she was fully aware of the source of her affliction and very conscious of its impact, she remained deeply affected by it throughout her adult years.

This next story shares a historical symmetry with the previous one and it relates to my original Karate Sensei from Okinawa, Master Kensei Taba. As a teenager he was forced to flee his beloved home on Okinawa, just after the Allies attacked in 1945. The freighter he was on was sunk by a submarine, forcing him to tread water for three days before being rescued. During this terrifying experience, where he witnessed many around him drown, he made a life defining promise to himself. If he were to survive, he would make himself as strong as possible so he would never feel so vulnerable as he did then, clinging to life in that open sea. He was rescued and years later, made good on his personal promise, selecting karate as the path to fortify himself. He went on to practise and teach the art throughout his later life and was widely respected and recognised as a Shihan – a genuine Master.

The saying, '*It is not so much what happens to you, but what you do with what happens to you*' has resonance here with both stories. Though sounding simplistic, it is not without wisdom. Do we allow past events to define us and if so, how? As this story of Master Taba illustrates, can traumatic experience eventually be harnessed and used to fuel positive outcomes?

Transforming behaviours

As the above stories illustrate, childhood experiences can have an immense and lasting impact on our lives, generating all sorts of belief systems and behaviours. Of these patterns, some are certainly sub optimal and linger on past their use by date. The following process provides a practical example of how you can reset and redirect unhelpful patterns of behaviour. Self-healing can be assisted by the application of a tool known as a 'pattern interrupt'. Though similar in function to the 'pause button', the purpose of this tool is to be used where there is an embedded form of behaviour you wish to transform.

⚒ *Toolbox: The pattern interrupt*

This tool is guided by a very simple intent – replacing a destructive pattern of behaviour with one which is constructive. To illustrate how this tool is applied, we will use passive aggression as an example of a pattern needing to be *interrupted*.

Passive aggression is frequently seen in conflict situations. In this context, it is used as a weapon to deliver nuanced expressions of anger as opposed to someone choosing to be open, assertive and direct. Behavioural patterns like this usually have their origins in childhood where individuals may not have felt safe in confidently asserting themselves, or expressing anger, and therefore learn the skills of doing so in a passive way. Sarcasm, cynicism, undermining and backstabbing are some of the tools belonging to this behavioural pattern.

Step 1: Identify and own it!

If passive aggression is a pattern you wish to move beyond, the first step is to recognise the situations where you find yourself being passive aggressive. Team meetings, family gatherings, dealing with people you don't like are some examples where passive aggression is frequently expressed. Once you've identified it, then own it. *Yes – that's me!*

Step 2: Reflection: Why do I behave this way?

The next step is to reflect on *why* you use it? The answer may be that you are fearful of direct confrontation. You may also be getting 'rewards' from such behaviour – a sense of vindication, a sense of being the victim, an opportunity to feel self-righteous and/or wronged and in a malicious way, enjoying the sense of inflicting psychological or emotional hurt on someone. Psychology informs us that individuals do not keep up patterns of behaviour unless there is some form of reward. Also, worth noting, the reward does not have to be positive or constructive as evident in the examples just listed.

Step 3: The pattern interrupt

The next time you are in a situation where something is said or done that would usually trigger your passive aggressive reaction, choose not to react to it. Instead, *interrupt the pattern* and 'pause' for a moment to ask yourself; What are my options here? Then take a breath ... And then another breath. Then choose a constructive response instead of one laced with passive aggression. You could: respond with a clarifying question; challenge back in a constructive, open manner; request some further time to reflect on what had been said to you or asked of you;

respond with genuine humour; agree with them and build on what was said; or offer a different perspective. These are just a few of the options before you in such contexts.

So what?

The *pattern interrupt* is a way to break from a pattern of behaviour. You consciously choose to do things differently and then act on the choice in a disciplined manner. You may have to bite your tongue for a while as it can take some time to bed in new *patterns* of behaviour. This simple action, sustained over time, can dramatically move you away from a destructive pattern. Although passive aggression was used to illustrate this process, it could be substituted for any other behaviour(s) you wish to change; conflict avoidance, arrogance, approval seeking, over-controlling, etc. You will need to apply discipline to establish new patterns and call on courage and be willing to give up the 'rewards' that you previously gained from such behaviours. And the upside to breaking these noxious patterns is a distinctive sense of personal growth and expansion. You will be also laying down new circuits (neural pathways) which will broaden your range of responses associated with challenging situations.

Tip

A primary reason the pattern interrupt approach can work, is that not only are you laying down new neural pathways, but you are also creating new habits. For example, a previous habit or default pattern may have been to employ passive aggression as a response of choice. You can now choose to form a new habit based on being direct, open and authentic. This approach has integrity and can build trust and strengthen relationships. Habits are very powerful in the manner in which they contribute to shaping personality. We tend to become what we habitually think, do and say.

A final observation before we move to the next chapter. Though we have journeyed through some of the very significant challenges that arise from the shadow side of the unconscious, please also keep in mind the very rich upside of the unconscious. This refers to the positive, life enhancing experiences you have stored there, the beliefs associated with these experiences and the affirmative feelings you hold about yourself and the world. Within your unconscious lies the wellspring of your creativity – a pool of potential inspiration resting there often undervalued and underutilised. We will visit this creative source in later chapters when we explore the flow states.

Chapter 7:
Being present – achieving mindfulness

Most people struggle to be present. They go to India and sit in Ashrams to 'get here now'. Most people live in fear because they project the past into the future. Michael (Michael Jordan) is a mystic – he was never anywhere else. His gift was not that he could run fast, or shoot a basketball. His gift was that he was completely present – and that was the differentiator.[1]

Mark Vancil

Mr. Duffy lived a short distance from himself ...

James Joyce

All we really have in terms of time is the ever-present moment. One moment followed by another and then another ... progressing endlessly and seamlessly in space and time until we finally shuffle off the mortal coil and then find out where that leads. There is only *this* moment in current space and time. Where specifically is your mind placing its attention this very moment? Your past only really exists in your memories, and the future... it never really arrives, for once it is here, it just becomes the current moment of Now. Regardless of such logic, many still spend much of their thinking time focused on past events or anticipating what will be or could be in the future. And such preoccupation can bring unhelpful implications both psychologically and biochemically.

According to the British National Institute for Mental Health, depression can be seen as ruminating in the past, whilst anxiety is ruminating in the future. This is a massive simplification, but it does point towards the inherent value in living life a day at a time and being engaged in the moments as they arrive. To help live like this, we need to be in the present moment or mindful, and that is where our exploration takes us next. Being mindful and being present are fundamentally the same thing and I will be using the terms interchangeably.

Two definitions to start.

> *Mindfulness involves the skillful use of attention to both your inner and outer worlds.*[2]

> *Mindfulness means paying attention to what is happening in the present moment in the mind, body and external environment, with an attitude of curiosity and kindness.*[3]

The inclusion of curiosity and kindness suggests a mindset of openness and one where the default setting is to non-judgement and empathy.

The nature of the mind is to think. Try not to think for a moment. (A pause for the exercise). You will probably realise you are thinking about not thinking. Even as you take your last breath in life your mind will still be chattering... Is this a good time to die? What about next Sunday after the match of the day...? The nature of your mind is to be highly active and resistant to efforts to still it. Another more realistic approach is to quieten the mind and take control of where your attention goes. This is the first step towards becoming mindful. And becoming mindful is the first step towards flow.

For the moment, what we attend to is reality.

William James

Being mindful is beyond just a technique; it points to a way to live life differently. When you become mindful, you have an increased capacity to consciously direct your attention.

What does this mean? I am 'here' now aren't I? Yes and No. The Buddhists call the mind the 'chattering monkey' – a brilliant description. Forever restless, moving from one topic to another, never quiet and rarely still. So yes, you are physically wherever your body is, but where is your mind? Practising being mindful helps take the chatter out of the monkey, quietening the grey matter and reduces the flow of discordant thoughts allowing you to be more fully present. Like a child chasing a butterfly, or a master musician in full flight, the mind is nowhere else but in the present. It is easy to bring your mind to the present. Keeping it there, however, is a tougher gig! It requires disciplined attention.

Big Tip

When you are in the moment, it is usually quite a pleasant place to be in.

A personal view I hold is that it is rare for people in the West to live mindfully, or to be fully present for any sustained length of time. Most of us are 'lights on, at home occasionally' running around, attempting to multitask, caught up in some form of a chaotic, frantic dance with life. When you encounter someone who is truly present, you tend to notice – usually because presence has impact. This is because you are meeting their mind, body and spirit. When you encounter someone who is truly present, it tends to draw you in. This idea is poignantly captured in the saying – presence invites presence ...

So, let's get present.

Exercise: Mindfulness – the practice

The intent of this exercise is to unplug the 'chattering monkey' and for you to be nowhere else apart from the 'moment' you find yourself in right now. Sitting down is probably the best option for this exercise, but if that is not possible then walking, standing, or wherever you are, will be fine. You need to be able to dedicate your attention to just one thing – and that is your breath. If your phone is nearby, switch it off.

Firstly, just become aware of your breath.

Just simply be aware of the rise and the fall of the breath in your body.

Notice where you can sense that you are breathing – in the nostrils, your throat, the rise and fall of your chest or through the expansion and contraction of your stomach. Just notice your breathing.

Now become aware of your feet on the ground. Feel a sense of connection with the ground.

Notice what part of your foot is making the strongest connection to the ground – either barefoot or wearing shoes, sense the core contact points where your feet connect with the ground.

If you are moving, simply apply the same focus to your feet as they move.

Notice the point of balance, where the contact is, where the weight tends to be distributed in your foot. This helps with a sense of grounding yourself, being connected physically and mentally with where you already are.

Become conscious of where your mind is – if there are thoughts, notice the thoughts, do not indulge them and effortlessly return to your breathing, your awareness of your feet on the ground ... as more thoughts arrive be aware of them ... and then just keep returning to the breath.

This is the exercise – just keep your attention now on your breath.

Be aware of the breath in your body and your feet on the ground ... Still the mind ... When you have thoughts, allow them to be there ... conscious of them like clouds on a bright day, but do not give them any further attention ... Be aware of them, but then bring your focus back to your breath and sense of connection with the ground. The same is true of feelings or sensation ... fear or fearful thoughts may arise, as may joyful ones, but you notice them very quickly and then – as with other sensations, just become aware of them and do not give it any more of your attention. Do not indulge in them. Keep coming back to your awareness on the breath.

Spend a few moments continuing this process – awareness of your breathing and connection to the ground. In this process you will arrive at a state of being mindful ... being present. Mindfulness is simply being conscious of where your attention is and where you wish to direct it. As thoughts, feelings and sensations arrive, you are mindful of them. There is no great mystery to this. Mindfulness just requires you to practise being present and being aware of where your attention is.

This is a simple and effective exercise based around a three-step cycle. The breath, being the point of focus, serves a similar function to that of a mantra in traditional Eastern based meditation. A mantra is a meaningless sound which is continually repeated with the intention of eventually quietening the mind by reducing thoughts. The mind cannot make any sense of the mantra because it is meaningless and after a while the thinking process begins to disengage and slows. Resting your attention on your breathing serves the same purpose. Eventually you will notice fewer and fewer thoughts till there will be time when there are no thoughts at all for periods of time. You expand the spaces existing between thoughts, which, when you think about it, is an interesting thought.

Keep your attention on your breath. When you have thoughts and you are aware that you are thinking these thoughts, just return to resting your awareness on your breathing. This is a simple cycle which you just need to keep repeating. You are now **meditating**.

A significant point to this exercise is the benefit of being able to calm the mind simply and quickly by focussing attention on the breathing cycle. If fears arise, or other strong emotions, or you feel your mind is really scattered, just do this exercise. It works. You will become calmer and you will be conscious of where your mind is and then have choice over where you wish to direct it.

A study published in 2018 in the Frontiers in Human Neuroscience sought to identify the reason as to why meditation and mindfulness practices are so beneficial.

> *The factor they pinpointed? The breathing, that complex mix of biochemistry and biomechanics that we take for granted. Specifically, slow diaphragmatic breathing. Because of its effects on stimulating and 'toning' the vagal (also known as the vagus) nerve, which influences cardiopulmonary fitness, immune function, stress, anxiety and executive functions. As they noted, simply paying attention to your breath tends to slow it and have a calming effect.[4]*

To get the full import of this paragraph above we need to back up and take a closer look at the function of this major cranial nerve.

> *The vagus nerve serves as the body's superhighway, carrying information between the brain and the internal organs and controlling the body's response in times of rest and relaxation. When the body is not under stress the vagus nerve sends commands that slow heart and breathing rates and increase digestion.[5]*

The research into vagal function points to practices such as meditation and mindfulness, which feature slow breathing, can create a form of 'respiratory biofeedback'. Techniques which include slow breathing and long exhalations 'will signal a state of relaxation by the vagal nerve, resulting in more vagal nerve activity'[6] and subsequently, relaxation is engendered. How simple can this be? By using the mindfulness practice of slowing both your breathing and heart rate, your vagus nerve is 'toned' which generates a relaxation response in the body. People experienced in using mindfulness techniques or meditation will have no need to be

convinced of the benefits of these breathing practices. They can feel it. It is reassuring however to know of the contemporary science which explains and validates how and why these techniques work.

Mindfulness and attention

Georgetown University Professor Cal Newport proposes in his book 'Deep Work'; 'attention' is the new key factor in competition. In his opinion:

'It's the brains that are able to mentally dismiss distractions that will be successful in the new economy. Not only because intellectual work will become even more prevalent, but

because it seems that the capacity for attention – in the current information chaos – is decreasing on a world scale.[7]

Does this idea resonate with you? Can you identify when you are effectively engaged with what is before you and when you are not? Can you notice the distinction in the quality of energy you bring with you to your work or other activities when your attention is focused? Those of you whose average day consists of a struggle to fight your way out of your Inbox just to get a few snatches of fresh air, moments before the rest of the day's back-to-back zooms roll on, may have cause to consider; *Is this brain of mine – which has taken millions of years to evolve to this finely tuned instrument – being effectively utilised here today?*

What often prevents a genuine sense of presence and connection in the moment is largely due to the propensity to try to multi-task. This refers to the distraction the mind experiences as it is bounced across multiple activities. Ample evidence shows that we are incapable of genuinely multi-tasking and in fact what we do is 'multi-switch'. This distribution of attention acts to prevent us from a sense of absorbed focus on a singular activity. According to research, productivity can be reduced by as much as 40% by mental blocks created when people switch tasks.[8]

To explore this further we will draw upon current research in the fields of neurobiology which helps explain why the mind is more effective when it is focused.

When you communicate with others, you can make yourself better heard by speaking louder or by speaking more clearly. Neurons appear to do similar things when we're paying attention. They send their messages more intensely to their partners, which compares to speaking louder. But more importantly, they also increase the fidelity of their message, which compares to speaking more clearly.[9]

To learn how to achieve higher levels of attention, it's best to look to the Masters and in this case, they come in the form of children.

Observe a child at play and you will notice an incredible degree of focused attention – or what we are calling mindfulness. When a child paints, or plays, or runs, or argues, or inspects a flower, just notice how present they are. How they pour their entire beings into everything they do. Even though a child's attention span quickly shifts from one thing to another, if you observe them closely you will notice their focus goes with them. Or as it is understood in martial arts, they *take their centre with them*.

The capacity children have to live in the moment can cause fault lines with their parents who over time have become used to having a widely dispersed attention. Working parents, at the end of a hard day's slog, whether it be locked up in a home office, or at a workplace, are usually weary, with their attention spread over the usual evening's 'to do list'. And who meets them at the door? A completely dialled on, living in the moment, attention craving, take-no-prisoner toddler. This child will be very sensitive to the level and quality of energy that is being directed towards them. They know when you are present with them because they will feel it. (Dogs are similar – they know when your mind is missing in action and when your heart is not in the patting you are giving them). A child's brain functions differently to that of an adult and is operating on different brainwave frequencies. Up until around eight years of age, children are accessing mainly alpha and theta brain waves which enable them to be very present. Alpha waves are associated with being singularly focused. From around eight, children start to show signs of beta brain wave activity which is associated with multi-switching and analytical thinking. If you have some form of a toddler or young child in your life, pay attention as they can teach you a lot about being in the present and being mindful. With practise, you can reclaim this wonderful quality of mindfulness that you also once had as a child.

> *Man is most nearly himself when he achieves the seriousness of a child at play.*
>
> *Heraclitus*

There is no other place to be apart from the current moment. When your mind wanders off on numerous trails of thoughts, it is just electrical signals firing off across the screen of your consciousness. You are still in the room, or in the meeting, your body sitting in the chair, nowhere else, it is just your mind taking off. When your mind drifts like this it can be immersed in delightful thoughts, or the opposite – thoughts or feelings associated with fear, anger or frustrations. This can happen regardless of how irrelevant such emotions may be in that specific situation. A brief story to illustrate this point.

I was washing dishes one morning, enjoying the warm water, soft bubbles and the sunlight playing on the window. The birds were chirping, the flowers flowering and the bees buzzing. I was feeling fine and just enjoying one of life's simple tasks. For some reason, a thought was triggered about an individual I really disliked. This thought acted like a magnet to other 'like thoughts' and in an incredibly short period of time, a whole queue of negative thoughts and feelings, related to this person and our history, were lined up vying for my attention. I became conscious of my jaw starting to clench and my stomach tighten, and I felt a certain charge of self-righteousness building towards this character. I was *indulging* in the dance of these thoughts and my anger was rising as a result. The awareness of the flowers, the warm water and bubbles was fading rapidly. These pleasant thoughts, from moments before, were overtaken by other, adrenaline inspired ones. My body was preparing for battle yet the only real challenge before me lay in completing the dishes. The villain was living on the other side of the city, no doubt completely oblivious to the war dance going on in my body/mind which was aimed at him. The water was still warm, the bubbles still there, the sunlight continued to dance, but I had lost connection with all that present-moment beauty.

The self-reinforcing loop

This story illustrates the reinforcing loop that occurs between thinking and feeling.

> *As you think certain thoughts, the brain produces chemicals that cause you to feel exactly the way you were thinking. Once you feel the way you think, you begin to think the way you feel. This continuous cycle creates a feedback loop called a state of being.*[10]

This brief passage is worth reflecting on, particularly if you are prone to being overcome by certain emotions and experience feelings of powerlessness. When the emotions start to build, or the angry thoughts begin to gather; stop, pause and choose other feelings to feel such as gratitude, compassion, empathy and other thoughts to think. The simple intent is to nip negative thinking or feelings in the bud before a self-reinforcing loop is triggered.

So what?

Regarding my dishwashing story, my thinking led to angry thoughts which took me away from what had been a pleasant morning. The thoughts were completely irrelevant to the moment, unhelpful and unwarranted. In relationship to this chain of events, you could substitute other core emotions such as fear, jealousy, guilt or sadness. As the feedback loop indicates, when we think in a certain way, it causes us to feel in a manner aligned and then the way we are feeling affects our thinking. This is great if the thinking and feeling is positive. What is worth reflecting upon is the frequency you give airtime to negative thoughts that can stimulate emotions which have no relevance with what is happening in the present moment. And what collateral damage is being done as these emotions generate the release of powerful chemicals?

Thoughts turn into chemistry as the information in chapter two details. When you are experiencing stressful emotions such as anger or fear, your body is releasing a series of hormones even if there is no threat present. Among these, adrenaline is frequently generated and if the stress is sustained, cortisol will eventually join the party. With these conditions in place, blood pressure and heart rate will also tend to rise. If sustained, these physiological and biochemical responses can be deleterious to your health. As chemistry expert Matt Church highlights:

> *'Adrenaline operates on a short-term emergency basis. Constant demands can lead to adrenal fatigue. If that happens cortisol begins to play a more significant part in managing the stress. Unlike adrenaline, the presence of cortisol has significant side effects including anxiety, edginess, fear or guilt.'* [11]

For those leading high-pressure lifestyles, whether it be in the business world or on the home front, pay attention to the above quote. If you are exposed to long periods of stress, there is a good chance your cortisol levels will be scaling up. This happens to compensate for declining levels of adrenaline which may have been exhausted getting the latest deadline in, striving to hit those excessively high sales targets or getting the three kids out the door for school over the preceding term. Researchers refer to cortisol as the ageing hormone due to its impact on overall wellbeing.

When you become conscious of feeling stressed, practise your mindfulness. When you are mindful you are more aware of what is happening in your mind and what feelings you are experiencing in your body. With this real time data feed, you can make conscious and timely adjustments as you navigate through the day. *Currently I feel really stressed, time for a walk ... I feel overwhelmed ... I need to delegate more and set clearer boundaries ... I am feeling flat ... time to hit the gym ... time to meditate ... etc.*

Exercise: Change your state

Our conscious mind is very capable of drifting from the present and dredging up all manner of memories, thoughts and feelings. This was illustrated in my dishwashing story. This next exercise is to do with taking control of the conscious mind – *becoming mindful* – and effectively changing your state.

If you are in a mood which is suboptimal – negative, fearful or aggressive – you can intentionally shift this to one which is more constructive. When you are feeling tired and frustrated, STOP and PAUSE for a few seconds and practise your mindfulness exercises. Find your breath, focus there for a few moments and choose what mood you wish to be in. This pausing acts as a *pattern interrupt*. I remember well a comment from a person who I was coaching years earlier, referring to this process of shifting state. His mindfulness practice enabled him to apply a 'full stop' to the end of his business day so that he did not take his 'work cloud' home with him.

A state change story

Many years ago, I was part of a small team tasked with helping improve the safety standards of an oil company operating rigs in the Bass Strait. To be able to set foot on the rigs, we first had to pass what was called the Heli Sea training. This training equipped you with the skills to be able to follow the correct procedures in the event of a helicopter crash at sea. You were not allowed on the helicopters or rigs without this accreditation. The training included firefighting, gas identification and safety drills. Overall, it was highly educational and fun. However, the Heli Sea training was the last qualification I needed that week and by the time this came around I was tired and a bit disengaged. This mood was to shift very quickly.

At the training venue, the Heli Sea instructor led us, by then fully dressed in overalls and steel capped boots, to the side of a large and very deep indoor pool. Centred in the pool was a strange set of machinery, attached to what appeared to be an aluminium cage, looking something like a half-finished submarine shell. He began to describe what we were about to attempt. We had to simulate a helicopter crash at sea, with a cabin full of fully dressed people, crammed in with seat belts fastened. The twist of this exercise, literally, is that we had to enter the cage, put our seat belts on and then wait as they sunk us into the water and subsequently rotated the cabin. All of this had to be carried out on a single breath. *"Excuse me ... Did you say just one breath ... and rotated? We will be suspended upside down, underwater?"* By now he had my full attention. This underwater rotation was to simulate how helicopters sink. We dutifully climbed on board, took a very deep breath and the cage was lowered four metres down, and then rotated. The escape process had to follow a very specific sequence – first, undoing our seat belts, releasing the doors, and then wait our turn for each seat to be vacated before we could step out of the cage and swim to the surface – all of this whilst on just one breath.

The point of this story is how quickly my state changed because it had to. Although I arrived tired and disengaged, by the time I had the first inkling of what I was about to face, my level of engagement switched dramatically. I became acutely present, focussing on each word the instructor uttered. It felt as if my life depended on these instructions.

So what?

If, under duress or necessity, you can effortlessly and very expediently change your state, you can do the same in any situation. Whether you are facing a challenging situation or just a conversation in a corridor at work or listening to a friend around a BBQ.

Achieving presence, being mindful is simply a choice.

This chapter has focused on the benefits of mindfulness and promoting the skills to enable you to reach this state. To close this chapter, I will draw upon a few lines from the very powerful and poignant story 'Chasing Daylight' by Eugene O'Kelly. The author was a former Chairman and CEO of KPMG in the United States. In 2005, aged 53, he was diagnosed with a terminal brain tumour.

The paragraph selected opens his book and the chapters that follow trace the closing months of his life. This final period of his life inspired the title, '*Chasing Daylight*'. On this journey, O'Kelly shares intimate insights on life and what he came to realise as truly important. The fact of having reached the pinnacle of the corporate world to be then confronted with a terminal disease, makes his insights all the more compelling. The lines below capture the wonder he experiences in just being able to hear and feel and partake in the simple, everyday happenings of life. As he is declining towards his death, he muses on the sensations he feels in the presence of a nearby fireworks display. Sounds that, prior to his diagnosis, he simply took for granted.

> *Through our living room window, we watched the fireworks launching from Macy's barge on the East River ... It is misleading to say I 'watched' the fireworks. On this night, July 4, 2005, the real highlight – at least for me – was not visual. True, I had developed vision problems, including blurriness and blind spots, which naturally diminished the glory of the spectacle, the arc and splash of the fireworks showering the sky outside our apartment window. But even had I been able to see more clearly the real thrill was the sound. Explosions booming off the surrounding skyscrapers, noise rumbling in the canyons of Manhattan's avenues, deep drumming like thunder reverberating throughout my body and my city. The sound was beautiful; it was eye opening. I would never have guessed the best part of fireworks could be something beside light and colour.*
>
> *You never know how you'll be surprised.*[12]

He died before he could complete his book. The final chapter, which is highly moving is written by his wife, Corrine. 'Chasing Daylight' is a celebration of life and an endorsement of the wonder and joy in those aspects of it that we so frequently take for granted.

Chapter 8: Embracing fear

Fear is excitement without the breath.

Fritz Perls

This quote makes for a bold statement. If you take a blood test when you are highly excited and another when you are highly fearful, and then compare the two, there would be considerable similarities between them. The point Fritz was making (*I believe*) is when you are feeling fear, recognise what is happening and *add breath*. Notice your breathing next time you are feeling fear and most likely what will be apparent is the lack of breath. Shallow breathing can act as a signal to fire up the adrenals. The simple feedback message is that you are under some form of stress, so the body acts accordingly and prepares a defense.

When you are experiencing fear and there is no genuine impending threat, it is most likely you are creating or at least contributing to this fear through your own thought processes. As an example, the apprehension you begin to feel regarding a difficult conversation or a tough situation you have to deal with can trigger a reaction anywhere from mild discomfort to extreme nausea and high anxiety. The mind in such situations fails to discern what is real and present and what is imagined. Either way, the system acts as if it is under threat and will direct the release of potent chemicals into your bloodstream.

> ... *much of what you see 'out there' is actually manufactured 'in here' by your brain ... Only a small fraction of the inputs to your occipital lobe (tasked with processing and analysing what our vision takes in) comes directly from the external world; the rest comes from internal memory stores and perceptual-processing modules. Your brain simulates the world – each of us lives in a virtual reality that is close enough to the real thing that we don't bump into the furniture. In the simulator, upsetting events from the past play again and again which unfortunately strengthens the associations between an event and its painful feelings. And to further add to this ... these mini movies (the scenarios playing out in our mind) are full of limiting beliefs.*[1]

Reflection

The information in this quote is quite extraordinary. As we bump around the world, within us, our own personal simulators are doing their best to interpret what is actually happening externally, through drawing upon stored data. Consider the potential for a poor or sloppy match between what is *really* happening in our external world and how our brain chooses to interpret it. As I write here, leaning on this solid oak table, I am confident I have enough accurate information to reliably process this experience as me, leaning on a sturdy table. However, within the thousands of moments that happen each day there is so much potential for poor matching by our internal *simulator*, particularly when we have very powerful belief systems in place and biases at play which we are largely unconscious of. Ascertaining clear intent to do with conversation, emails, texts or tweets, as well as accurately interpreting facial expressions, voice tonality and body language represent examples of how difficult this process can be. Do we notice the changes in the world and the people around us, yet keep referencing old files? What is the opportunity cost of failing to consciously update our internal software with new perceptions and new ways of looking at life and the people who share it with us? And regarding perceptions of self, do we keep drawing upon stored data and old beliefs or is it time for a spring clean and renewal?

As the preceding paragraphs highlight, the process by which we interpret reality is by its nature, unreliable and frequently flawed. Therefore, our ability to be present and conscious of where our mind is dwelling and what thoughts it is generating, is highly important. As Professor Csikszentmihalyi offers;

> *'Control of consciousness determines the quality of life.'*

This statement manages to be both provocative and inspiring simultaneously. Provocative because it highlights the personal accountability we hold to affect and shape our lives. And inspiring, for the very same reason.

Choice

Where you place your attention, every moment of each day, is your choice as are the observations, judgements and responses that ensue. I recently watched a documentary on the ancient city of Homs which has been largely destroyed by the Syrian War. The scenes revealed acres of a devastated, desolate city, the detritus of war everywhere, not a building intact and destroyed property and broken glass everywhere. The camera turned to a group of boys who were playing amongst the rubble. They were asked by the journalist what they thought about their city. Their response – *we love our city; we think it is very beautiful and we love living here*. This response was a surprise and a delight and reminded me, with great clarity and poignancy, we constantly have choice as to how we respond to what is before us. I was also reminded of how easy it is to transfer our projections onto others. In the case of the boys, I was expecting a tale of woe.

Exercise: Breathing process to help calm fears

This next exercise is intended to help you *'control your consciousness'* and move beyond the grip of fear and the feelings which accompany it. If fear is not a concern, this exercise can also serve as way to relax.

To undertake this exercise, find a quiet place and plan for a few moments in solitude.

Step 1 – Become present

Where are you sitting, lying? What is immediately before you – a table, a window, a carpet etc? Just notice what is around you – just the everyday objects of life. Notice the quality of light where you are – is it artificial light, or sunlight? Notice where the shadow falls. Notice the different shades of colours around you. Notice where your body is making contact with what you are sitting or lying on. What specific part of your body is in contact (back, backside, legs, etc) ... notice all this taken-for-granted information. As you are paying close attention to this sensory input, you are drawing yourself into the 'present'.

Step 2 – Awareness of the sensations in your body

Having established a degree of comfort in where you are, now put your attention into your body. Spend a few moments reflecting on *how* you are feeling. What sensations are you experiencing? What emotions are you feeling – joy, sadness, fear? If you describe these sensations as fear, where are you feeling this fear? How is it registering in your body? Examples could be tight stomach, clenched jaw, high heart rate, feelings of nervousness, etc. Allow your attention to stay for a moment in these areas of your body so that you can clearly register what feelings and sensations are showing up.

Step 3 – Add breath

Now place your awareness on your breath and just breathe naturally, nothing excessive or forced, nor too shallow. Place a hand on your belly, just below your belly button and breathe down, effortlessly into this place, so that this resting hand may rise and fall gently with the in and out breath. Never force the breath. Just keep this cycle going for a few minutes, just resting your awareness on the rise and the fall of your breath. At this phase this is all you have to do. Just be aware of your breath in your body. The rise and the fall, the rise and the fall ...

Step 4 – Release the tension

Now put your awareness to where you are feeling 'fear' – that is if you are still feeling fear, for often this simple breathing exercise calms the body/mind very effectively. If the fear is still there, simply rest your awareness on the sensation (fear) that you are experiencing. If it is a tight or churning stomach, nervous legs, rapid heart rate, etc, just put your attention there and *release the tension with your breathing*. On the exhalation, release tension and on your inward breath, breathe in relaxation. One pointer – keep the exhalation longer than the in breath. If you are breathing in for the count of four seconds, exhale to the count of eight. This will help 'tone' the vagus nerve as previously detailed in Chapter 7. Just keep this simple cycle going whilst ever you feel fear. Notice where the fear is showing up, put your awareness on it and allow this breathing process to release the tension. There is nothing forced about this breathing. The key is simply to breathe naturally and deeply into your abdomen. In martial arts this is called breathing into your *hara* – your life centre. Just keep this process going until you experience a tangible release of the discomfort in your body.

After you use this exercise a few times, you will notice your body/mind will quickly respond to the process once it is triggered. You will be able to get in the groove, or in this case, to a relaxed state, quickly as you tone your vagus nerve. Regular use of this technique will act to keep firing and wiring these specific neural connections associated with relaxation.

Experiencing fear but don't know where it has come from?

Most of the time when the physical impact of fear is experienced – tight jaw, cramping stomach, fast heartbeat, short breath even scaling up to some form of anxiety or even panic – there will be cognition regarding the source of the fear. For example, it could be caused by thinking of a presentation you have to give, or a tough conversation coming your way. But what about the times you are feeling fear and you don't know why and cannot attribute it to a specific reason?

Research carried out by Dr Lilliane Munjca-Parodi identified how the amygdala can be triggered by things which we are unconscious of, including smells.[2] A fight, flight or freeze reaction is activated in the mind/body but the cause of this reaction does not register on our conscious mind. The sensation of fear is felt but the cause unknown. To mitigate the impact of fear does not require you to be aware of its source. The previous exercise will help if you are someone who commonly experiences fear but have no clear cognition of its source.

So – when you are feeling fearful but don't know why, just follow Steps 1 through to 4 from the previous exercise. The point to this process is to be mindfully aware of what is taking place in your body. By identifying the areas where fear is having a physical impact, you are no longer an unconscious recipient but an active player in your own process. You are having the emotion; the emotion is not having you! (If however, you find yourself regularly pushing the piano behind the front door, sharpening wooden stakes and donning a Rambo bandana, you may need additional help beyond this guide).

Conscious attention

When conscious attention is applied to sensations of fear, the higher centres of the brain get to play a more involved role and can help to calibrate what is taking place biochemically in the mind/body. The amygdala may be firing up, but when rational thinking is applied (usually helped by the mediating influence of the hypothalamus) the most likely result is a calming of your sympathetic nervous system. As mentioned previously, this is called *focussing your attention* or having *conscious attention*. Try it and see what happens. You can do this anywhere, anytime.

🧰 *Toolbox: Hooking your attention*

When your attention drifts and you know you need to focus, find something you can *hook* it to. Examples of this may be the grain in the table on which you are working, the colour in a painting hanging in a room or where light is landing from the window. For a few brief moments bring your attention to this specific point. If it were the grain in the woodwork, just notice the subtle variations and change in tones. Once you have your attention *hooked*, you are then able to direct it at will. This is good training for developing your mindfulness and a helpful exercise if your notice your attention drifting towards fearful thoughts. Hook it and bring it back to the present.

Being aware of your awareness

You do not have to engage with unhelpful or fearful thoughts, just notice them. Be aware of them. Notice how one thought tends to attract similar thoughts; in the case of fear, how fearful thoughts, act to generate other fearful thoughts. This can be likened to playing middle C on a piano which causes all the other notes of C to quietly resonate with it. You may also notice which thoughts tend to dominate. If you so choose, you can determine to have different thoughts. Alternatively, instead of indulging in fearful thoughts you can also engage your mind in something constructive like a physical activity, or a creative project, or you could head out the door and connect with nature which is the greatest of healers.

So what?

The capacity to become *aware of your awareness* is a very useful skill and *practice*. Instead of being so absorbed by your thoughts, you just notice them. In doing so you are able to recognise that your thoughts are just something occurring in your mind – not something taking place in the physical environment you are in. This is known as meta cognition which is defined as;

> *Awareness and understanding of one's own thought processes*
>
> *Oxford languages*

Thoughts are a touch like fireflies. Just a flash of electrical energy across the screen of your consciousness. When you get practised at this meta cognition, or witness consciousness, you can quickly assess if the thoughts you are having are helpful or not and, if required, re-orientate your thinking to something which is more constructive. That is a good example of being mindful and underscores why this practice is described as the *skilful* use of attention. A further suggestion is to keep reminding yourself that in the 'present', perceived threats are just that, perceived, they are not real. In most circumstances, the *present* is usually quite pleasant and unthreatening. And if the fear does persist, invite it along for the ride, welcoming it as energy, a friend, a companion. Embrace it!

Chapter 9: Reframing

Our key to transforming anything lies in our ability to reframe it.

Marianne Williamson

On the journey towards experiencing more flow in life, actively practising the skill of being mindful is a critical step. Once you have arrived in the present moment and you have harnessed the attention of your mind, you are now positioned to direct it. What influences where and how our mental energy is directed are the type of 'frames' we use. The shift from fear to flow may at times simply require you to *reframe* what you are experiencing.

🧰 Toolbox: Reframing Part 1

Each day brings with it events and experiences which require your attention. In the process of interpreting these experiences, that is, making sense of them, you choose certain angles or perspectives to view them from as well as assigning them to some form of context. This process can be likened to a picture framer selecting where they will place the frame on a photo. They are very conscious of where they are applying the frame – what is in, what is out, what is highlighted. When you view a situation, take a certain angle of interpretation, that is, 'frame' something in a certain way, the choice is usually driven from the unconscious. Why? Because it usually happens automatically. This can cause problems due to our own unconscious bias. To give an example, in a thirty minute presentation you stumbled once. As you review your presentation, this one stumble becomes the focal point of your attention. This is how you have 'framed' this experience. In doing this you will be disregarding or diminishing your efforts in the other twenty-nine minutes. This is an expression of unconscious bias, as you are habitually defaulting to a pattern of personal self-criticism, where 'what went wrong' heads the list.

This common storyline highlights the perils of 'selective' framing for it is often what is not in the frame, the additional data or different viewpoints – which could tilt the perception of an experience from a negative to one which is positive or enables you to see things that you had not seen before. The presentation has not changed, you just need to realise you can choose to shift the focus to the successful 29 minutes and not allow your inner critic to dine out on that one poor moment. This is not about being overly positive or optimistic, but more about establishing a balanced perspective.

If you are prone to excessive self-judgment, try the following process next time you begin to go down that unhelpful neural pathway. Take a situation where you have just done something – taken the lead in the Opera, baked a cake or pitched a tent. On completion of the task, before the inner critic unleashes, simply pause, and take a breath. Then before you begin your usual default to self-demolition, ask yourself the question, *'What did I do well?'* Undertake a high-level evaluation of what was positive in what you did. This is taking an *active position*. Passive would be handing the microphone over to the inner critic. This active position helps build confidence by identifying where value was created. The next question – *What could I have done better,* or *how will I do things differently in the future?* Reflect on these questions and take a few mental notes where improvement can be achieved. These questions collectively create a simple and *balanced* evaluation process. In essence, a reality check. One that helps avoid self-flagellation and, in the process, builds confidence.

A point of caution. Others can set framing traps that we can inadvertently walk into. Recently we approached a car dealer to test drive a new family car. I asked the dealer the benefits of trading in our current car versus selling it privately. His framing was classic. *'Well, if you want a bunch of strangers coming to your home and crawling all over your car and just kicking tyres... by all means go for it and best of luck with trying to sell it that way'.*

I remember suppressing my laughter. I was going to suggest he could have reframed it differently but chose not to. We did sell it privately and made five thousand more than his best offer.

So what?

Where you put the frame your attention will follow? Being attentive to where and how you frame events, experiences and people is a useful attribute.

To help with this, here are some useful questions.

- How am I framing this (situation, person, event, etc) and is this the most appropriate angle to choose? If not, what is a more appropriate frame?

- Am I being overly pessimistic or optimistic and do I need to reassess?

- Do I need to broaden the frame or reduce it and sharpen the focus?

- Are there opportunities I have failed to see because they exist outside my current frame of reference?

Back in the first decade of this century, I was introduced to a novel approach to purchasing real estate. I was hopeful, optimistic and keen to avoid missing out on the great real estate boom sweeping the Eastern states; this is how I chose to frame it. The potential downside of the investment was given scant attention. I really paid for that lack of perspective. The value of the house went nowhere but south about three minutes after my purchase and continued in that direction for the next ten years. With great skill, I had managed to slip in at the top of the market. On review, what became obvious was my assessment was overly optimistic and I had also fallen victim to the machinations of *confirmation bias*. This bias has the effect of directing attention towards information and data which supports an existing viewpoint and filters out information which could counter or challenge that view.

Tip

Pay attention to the potential for confirmation bias playing a role in how you frame things. It can be very subtle. When it comes to significant decisions, either in your personal or professional life, get a trusted friend to stress test your thinking. This simple action could save you a lot of money, heartache and misery. In this stress test, keep a lookout for another form of unconscious bias which shows up as making a decision in terms of *what* to do before getting a clear understanding as to the *why*. For those of you who have a default setting to ACTION you may want to reflect on this dynamic of placing the *what before* the *why*. Frequently these two forms of unconscious bias – confirmation bias and the what before the why – interact with each other, forming a potentially deadly combination. You plan on a course of action before effectively understanding the why you are doing it and then you seek out information to confirm you have made the right decision.

⚒ *Toolbox: Reframing Part 2 – Optimism and Pessimism*

According to Martin Seligman (Professor of Psychology at the University of Pennsylvania and author of '*Authentic Happiness*' and '*Learned Optimism*'), having an attitude to life more aligned to optimism, rather than pessimism, can help keep your immune system robust, contribute to experiencing greater satisfaction levels in life and in general help you 'flourish'.[1] Significantly, optimists tend to outlive pessimists. (*The good news for pessimists relating to this data is that you will need less Super*). These findings are underpinned by decades of research he and others in the field have undertaken. This next section will cherry pick a few gems from this research to build on our central theme relating to the benefits of being mindful. This information, if applied with diligence, can be life changing.

Pessimists and optimists tend to have distinctive approaches when it comes to interpreting their experiences in life.

The three P's

When something happens, which could be interpreted as 'bad', pessimists tend to explain it as;

- Personal – it's my fault

- Pervasive – this is everywhere

- Permanent – it will always be this way

Optimists tend to explain 'bad' or negative events as relating specifically to the situation, limited to the situation and of short duration, till a more positive change of events takes place.

When something 'good' happens, pessimists have the perspective that it is;

- Personal – what has this got to do with me?

- Pervasive – it really does not mean anything anyway

- Permanent – things will go back to normal tomorrow

Optimists take the flip side of this – positive events are personal, they are pervasive, (everywhere) and they are long lived.

If you have further interest is this area, Seligman's significant body of research is a rich field to explore.

Try this as a helpful exercise. Pause after something either really 'good' or 'bad' has happened to you and see how you explain this event to yourself. This is what is referred to as your *'explanatory style'*. Did you explain this event, more in the light of a pessimist, as outlined above, or more towards the style of an optimist?

So what?

These few lines cannot possibly convey the depth of information that is covered in Seligman's work on this subject. Hopefully though, it might inspire you to do some further exploration. As a snapshot, you are not stamped in your DNA as a pessimist or an optimist, or something in between. As you would appreciate, there are upside and downside traits in both. What is helpful is the recognition that you can alter the lens, or in other words, *reframe*, how you perceive events. If you lean more towards pessimism, and; you would like to enjoy life more fully, have a healthier body, a more resilient immune system, as well as potentially live longer and laugh more often – then consider shifting towards the optimist's explanatory style; the fact that positive events and experiences are *personal*, they do happen *everywhere*, and you may just need to look harder and longer, or in different places, or with a different lens to find them.

🧰 *Toolbox: Reframing Part 3 – Catastrophising*

Catastrophising refers to an irrational way of thinking about something in a manner which represents it as being far worse than it actually is. This can relate to something that has happened or something that could happen. The word itself captures the notion of a *disproportionate reaction* to something or some situation. If you are someone who does catastrophise, you may find benefit in following these uncomplicated reframing steps.

When you recognise you are catastrophising, you need to first pause and take a breath or two. Then *reflect* for a few moments.

- A useful question to ask yourself; What is a *fair and rational assessment of what has happened* (or could happen)?

- If the event is from the past, you could then ask yourself; *What went well, where do I need to change and what do I need to learn?*

- If the event is future based, the questions could be around; *What can go well, what can I learn and where will I find enjoyment in this experience? What do I need to do to ensure the success of this endeavour? What is there about this opportunity that excites me?*

Questions to oneself are effective as they require you to reflect and get perspective. An example of this is when an opportunity presents and you begin to feel a sense of fear. Perspective will help you decide whether this opportunity is for you to take or if a more appropriate choice is to let this pass. Perspective is the antidote. Are the Visigoths storming the Citadel or is this just a minor skirmish in meeting room 12?

So what?

It is helpful to notice when your reactions or fears might be *disproportionate to* what is happening or could happen. Remember what you *fire* gets wired. If your thinking is made up of repetitive and negative thought patterns such as in catastrophising, your health may also be impacted; high stress levels, poor sleep, constant feelings of anxiety, etc.

> *Any brain changes are at the expense of other changes. The development of these parts of our brain that effortlessly trigger anxiety, it is at the detriment of the ones that aid calmness and confidence ... it is not enough to just stop anxiety in any given moment which is often people's focus. The anxiety wiring is still there and waiting to be triggered. We need to create competitive wiring. We need to create specific wiring of what we want to achieve which is 'competitive wiring' to the problem. Without this we loop endlessly in anxiety with no neural pathway to take us forward.*[2]

Ian Cleary PhD

This is a very compelling piece of information. Preventing yourself from indulging in catastrophising represents a constructive step. In addition to this, you can then lay down some new competitive wiring which has an affirmative message. Consider. *What are some ways you can start to think differently about situations, people, events that cause you to feel anxious? What are some new thought lines you can create?* What will help with this process is to create new habits. James Clear, in his inspiring book *'Atomic Habits'*[2] highlights the significance of making small daily decisions to nurture the process of change and improvement. He focuses upon creating new habits as an enabler of constructive change. This process to create new habits is, at core, a reframe.

🧰 Toolbox: Reframing Part 4 – Creating new habits

Almost every habit you have, good or bad, is the result of many small decisions you have made over time. And if this is true, if the problems you are facing now are the results of thousands of small decisions made over the course of time, wouldn't it then be logical to employ the same process to correct them? [3]

James Clear is emphatic regarding his approach to laying down new habits. You need to avoid *trying not to do a bad habit* (eating when you are stressed) but instead find a new habit which overrides the 'bad' or destructive one. In this case of opening the fridge door when under stress, what would be a healthier, more effective way to deal with it? Possibly some meditation or mindfulness or indulge yourself in a few moments of exercise. You could make such a response into a *new* and positive habit. Daily habits, for example tiny routines that are repeatable, are the actions which enable transformation to take place.

✄ *Toolbox: Reframing Part 5 – Disputation*

When experiencing fear, it is useful to pause and just observe how your own internal narrative spools out. What is it you are telling yourself and most importantly, are you telling yourself the truth? On a trip to New Zealand many years ago, I was given the opportunity to partake in what would have been my first bungee jump. I declined. Yes, there was definitely fear there, but my primary reason for not leaping and screaming into the void had more to do with the rationale that it was not worth the potential of relocating my retinas several centimetres from where they are meant to be. Though I certainly felt fear at the idea of the jump, my decision not to, was based primarily on logic and a rapid assessment of risk versus reward.

So what?

The key point here relates to the internal narrative you are having when you are not telling yourself the truth. Unlike my reasoning regarding the bungee jump, I have an irrational fear of technology. As Zoom meetings increasingly become the new norm, my internal story is full of worse case scenarios of how I am likely going to crash the whole gig by hitting the button not to be hit. This is an example of where the tool of *disputation* can show its worth.

Disputation, which draws upon the principles of Cognitive Behaviour Therapy (CBT) refers to the ability you have to consciously challenge or 'dispute' negative or unhelpful thoughts with a perspective which is primarily rational. In my case with technology, it is irrational. To date I have led many successful virtual meetings and workshops and not blown any up. And yet still I notice a tendency to give airtime to my inner critic's default to worst case scenario. The inner critic, that most of us have, has a default setting to negativity and judgement and thrives in diminishing its host – which is you. In balance, it is fine to be self-critical. This is part of the path to learning and developing. The problem is this entity is often given a disproportionate amount of airtime and influence. It needs a counterweight, and fortunately you have one. You may not be aware of this, but somewhere in the back blocks of your psyche, undernourished and unloved, exists your *inner cheer squad*. You need to bring this team into the light and give them some airtime and nourishment and listen to their story with as much attention as you give the inner critic.

We will use a scenario to illustrate this interplay between your critic and your cheer squad. An opportunity has arisen for you to get a promotion at work. When this happens, you become aware that your thinking is defaulting to doubts and fears: *I am not good enough... Others are frontrunners... My peers will reject me ... I will fail ... and on and on.*

Holding a narrative along such lines is not helpful and it has the capacity to erode your confidence at a time when you are required to shine. If you were to employ the tool of *disputation* and turn it on your own negative thinking, it could run something like this; *I am good enough and I have proven this over many years. I have no specific evidence that others are front runners, and my peers may in fact be happy for me if I do get the promotion.*

How simple is this? You are just *disputing* your own negative or limiting thoughts and replacing them with a more balanced, rational and affirmative line of thinking. Over time this can be a very effective way to reduce unwarranted, self-limiting or self-destructive thoughts.

Disputation is not about overriding negative thoughts with an inflated or unrealistic, positive view. It is about helping establish in a sustainable way an accurate assessment of a situation.

⚒ *Toolbox: Reframing Part 6 – Acceptance*

Often what challenges the capacity to be present is a failure or reluctance to 'accept' how things really are – how one's life currently is unfolding. Acceptance can be a powerful friend.

> *'Acceptance is like finding that firm foothold. It's a realistic appraisal of where your feet are and what condition the ground is in. It doesn't mean that you like being in that spot, or that you intend to stay there. Once you have a firm foothold, you can take the next step more effectively. The more fully you accept the reality of your situation – as it, here and now, is – the more effectively you can take action to change it.'[4]*
>
> *Dr Russ Harris*

I really value this quote, often sending it to people who are either in a challenging situation or at some form of a crossroads in their life. The practise of pausing and coming to terms with *'what is'* as opposed to what *could be or should be*, is a required step in learning to live in the present. Achieving a level of acceptance can also help dissipate feelings of frustration, regret and anger. The reason *acceptance* is positioned as a reframe is because it requires a shift of focus away from what is desired, to what is current and real. Having your feet firmly planted in your current reality, as uncomfortable or frustrating as it may be, is the best place to make effective decisions regarding your next steps.

Our *next steps* pick up on this practice of having a 'firm foothold' and being grounded. We call this skill being centred.

Chapter 10:
Learning to centre – creating a dynamic stillness

Being centred is when the mind, body and spirit come to a unified central focus, regardless of external stimuli ...

Thomas Crum – Aikido Master

Time past and time future,
What might have been and what has been
Point to one end, which is always present.'

T.S. Eliot

Principle: Becoming centred

The above definition by Thomas Crum, poignantly captures the sense of being centred. When you are centred, you feel it. You may not be aware of your 'spirit' entwined with your mind and body, but you do feel focused, alert, energised and resourceful. A state of being centred will help you deal with what life throws at you – be it an angry customer, a gnarly wave, an unhappy boss or a tantrum-tossing toddler. What distinguishes being centred from being present is the level of energy at call. Bullfighters are more than just mindful when they face off to a charging half-ton beast. They are poised, ready to spring into evasive action in the blink of an eye. They are centred and their lives are dependent upon staying that way.

In the diagram below, the dot represents the centre, the still point, surrounded by the vital energy of life.

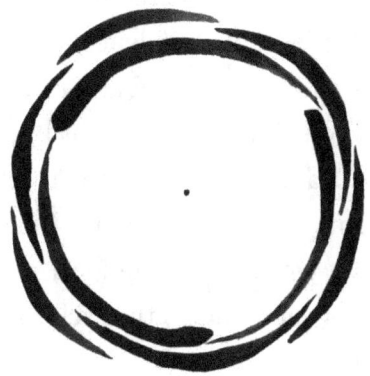

Centre is not a place; it is a state of being.

The value in being able to centre yourself extends beyond the realm of such extreme pursuits as bullfighting or the martial arts; it is applicable to all walks of life. Being centred can mean anything from having relaxed attention in the moment, to an extreme situation, such as being physically attacked in the street whereby you must immediately direct all your energy and resources towards self-preservation.

Maybe you haven't faced charging bulls before, or been attacked in the streets, but you have experienced being centred. Probably far more than you realise. Driving in wild and dangerous weather you are forced to focus your attention and your body responds by becoming highly energised and alert. Compare this situation to one of a leisurely drive around the suburbs on a Sunday afternoon. You are in the same body and the same car, but your *state* is very different. Those who surf or ski understand centredness. It is critical for success, for without it, gravity will prevail. In these pursuits, your mind/body awareness takes up residence in the moment and in the few metres before you. If you listen to the fearful voices inside your head, your attention is distracted, you lose your flow and you fall off the wave or you hit the snow. Riding a horse requires centredness. The horse beneath you reads your level of confidence. It can sense your control or your tentativeness and will respond accordingly. In simple terms, the centred state allows individuals to bring forward their best; Michael Jordan in a slam dunk, Pavarotti reaching for those final notes in Nessun Dorma or your neighbour, fully engaged with their children as they play with them in the local park. Centredness can also be witnessed at key moments in the cycle of life, with birth being a potent example of this.

The process of bringing a life into this world requires a remarkable fusion of mental, emotional and physical energy. In this most profound of processes, the external world loses all significance, allowing the lifeforce to concentrate on the mighty task of giving wings to a new life. In the context of birth, centredness just happens. The situation requires it, and the mind/body knows how to respond.

This centred 'state' is also clearly evident in the action of saving life. Surgeons are frequently required to deal with extremely complex operations which may require many hours of highly focused attention. A common practice among these eminent professionals is to follow a set of rituals to prepare for surgery. Laying out their instruments in a particular way, engaging in calming breathing exercises or listening to music are examples of this. The result of these rituals helps them get into their most effective '*state*' – in other words, this is how they centre themselves.

This process of using rituals to create an optimum *state* is common among master musicians. Edith Piaf, the famous French singer, had her own unique way of finding her centre. Prior to releasing her first note she would step on stage, make strong and deliberate eye contact with her audience and then move to the microphone stand where she would swivel her hips, as if twisting her feet into the floorboards. This was her version of getting centred and connecting with her audience. With this connection to the ground and to her audience in place, she would then raise her arms and begin to sing, filling the room with her signature voice. What has frequently been written about her ascribes to the remarkable level of power she generated from such a diminutive frame, exhibited in terms of volume, energy and presence. Whitney Houston attracted similar feedback. This highlights a salient point. You don't have to have a large and dominating physical body to project presence and power. You can achieve this regardless of your size and being able to centre will certainly help.

So what?

You may be thinking what is the key point here? I have no plans to be a surgeon, singer or bullfighter. The simple idea, as reflected in these examples, is that being able to centre allows your best self to show up when it is needed. You could be making a major presentation, participating in a sporting event, on a first date, or running a teenager's party. Being centred will give a platform for your best self to show up and shine.

In the East, the principle of being centred is well understood and is found in many of their cultural disciplines, particularly martial arts. In the Japanese language, the word denoting centre, is *hara*. According to tradition, the hara is situated a few inches below the navel. The hara is not some physical place, but more a centre where the energetic fields in the body coalesce. Though difficult to describe, or verify in scientific terms, the hara can be viewed as the focal point of one's connectivity; physically, emotionally and spiritually to life.

> *As far as the Japanese are concerned, the centre of balance or the centre of gravity in the body is the point which relates man to the earth, to nature, to the cosmos, and is therefore man's actual nucleus in terms of physical as well as psychic terms.*[1]
>
> Michael Random

The Japanese term hara *kiri* (to cut) refers to the ritual suicide of the samurai, where the 'hara' or life centre or life force, is cut by a sword forcibly driven into the belly and then drawn upward. According to tradition, the further the sword was drawn upward, the more courageous the samurai. A more pleasant association of the word hara lies with the poetic translation of the hara as a place in the body *where the elixir of life is created and where it rests.*

In the West, we are not so poetic; our everyday language however does indicate the connection we have with an inner core. We often talk about 'gut feel', 'gut instinct', whether we can 'stomach something' or 'digest something' or have the 'guts' (courage) to do something.

In Chinese martial arts as well as their traditional healing systems such as acupuncture, this 'centre' is called the tan-t'ien. In Indian teachings, the chakra or energy wheel, which is just below the navel, is known as Svadhisthana. Taking a Western engineering lens, we could say that the hara area, or just below the navel, is where our centre of gravity is situated. Martial artists, boxers, dancers and athletes well understand the importance of using their centre to help create their overall stability and to project both poise and power.

Disciplines such as karate, kendo, judo, tai chi, aikido and kung fu all have specific techniques which are designed to enable us to be able to both draw from and strengthen the hara – or centre. With the hara correctly engaged, there is less need to use sheer muscle strength to express power. This is because when you are centred your body is relaxed, your breathing is deep and calm and the energy within moves with greater ease as it is not restricted by tight, tense muscles. As practitioners age and their muscle mass declines, the connection with these more subtle, internal energies becomes more important. You may have recognised this journey, the path from youthful exuberance to eventual mastery, as a theme in many martial arts movies. The old silver-haired masters, long past their youth, rely on experience, skill and their inner powers to vanquish their opponents and have no need to flex and flash their muscles. They draw their power from their centre.

The energy which circulates through the hara has many names, among them the better known are ki, chi, or prana. Though these terms relate to the breath they are referencing more than just breathing as they also encompass subtle energy fields. This is the 'breath of life' that circulates throughout our body and brings wellness and vitality. In the East, being unwell is often related to having weakened ki and to improve one's health is to rejuvenate your ki, or as in acupuncture, find out where your chi is blocked and help restore the rightful *flow* of this energy.

The Tai Chi martial artist began his exercise standing naturally erect, his body completely relaxed, knees slightly bent, feet rooted to the earth, which was the source of all strength, the spine straight but not rigid, and the head held upright, as if suspended by a skyhook, so that the shen or spirit was drawn up to heaven. The mind or intention directed the chi to the tan-tien, the centre of gravity, a spot located just below the navel between the stomach and the backbone. Standing in this way, the Tai Chi player is in touch with the three powers – the upright head connected him with the power of heaven, the rooted feet with the power of earth, and the chi (life force) in the tan-tien (centre or hara) connected both of these to the centre of man.[2]

Whatever your perspective on Eastern cosmology, a Western physio, chiropractor or osteopath would have trouble faulting the dictates of this teaching; feet connected and grounded, knees unlocked, straight and supple spine and head held firm and upright.

Whether you believe in the existence of subtle fields of energy within and around us, or not, the practice of centring will still be beneficial. The reason is simple, as it is based on breath and, depending on how you are breathing, you can create either calm or discord within (and around you). As explored previously, when feeling fear or some level of stress, breathing tends to be shallow, circulating primarily in the upper regions of the lungs. This acts to stimulate the adrenals, as it is indicating the body is in some form of stress, which in turn, triggers the Fight or Flight response. This can be anything from a minor reaction to a major panic attack. When relaxed, the opposite happens, where deep, *effortless* breathing can really help bring about a sense of calm.

Projecting presence and gravitas

If you need to be able to project qualities such as presence and gravitas, learning how to centre will be a helpful step. I am not referring here to some ability to come across as *Presidential* or some corporate or political heavyweight. I am referring to your *personal* version of what is presence and/or gravitas. You may be heading up a corporation, coaching a team, leading a project or running a family. Regardless of what situation you find yourself in, being able to project presence is a useful attribute to have. Why? Because you will be noticed and it is more likely that people will pay attention to you. Without it you can go unnoticed and just blend into the background and that may happen in the board room, the sporting field or the dinner table.

The word gravitas has a Latin origin, which refers to *possessing a solemn dignity*. This was a coveted characteristic for leaders of the time when Rome ruled. The meaning has not changed greatly over the centuries. In today's corporate landscape a frequently required attribute of a senior leader is *Executive presence*. This is synonymous with gravitas.

Gravitas is not an arrogance, nor a superiority and it cannot be fabricated, as there is an authentic quality to it which defies pretence. Gravitas is not about positional power, more about personal power. People who have it tend to possess high levels of self-confidence, are 'comfortable in their skin' and are very present and grounded. Others will tend to notice those who have this quality – this energy walks into the room with them. A friend of mine acted as a junior lawyer on the team supporting Nelson Mandela during his final years in prison. He said when Mandela entered the room, though still a heavily guarded prisoner and dressed in drab clothing, he projected gravitas and authority. The effect, according to my friend, was that everyone knew immediately who was in charge.

You don't need to be famous, or high up in the executive suite to have gravitas. Many years ago, as I was back-packing around Thailand, the train I was travelling on, broke down at a station. My primary view, for many hours, was of a man, with a small stand, selling peanuts. Nothing remarkable about that apart from this person's energy. He just had a powerful presence, which I found intriguing. As he engaged with his customers, he projected a field of stillness and centredness which I still reflect upon today.

So, if you feel you would like to dial up your gravitas quotient, how do you go about it? The baseline has already been established in your practice of being *present*. Once present you can then choose to centre yourself. When you operate from a point of being centred you can choose what kind of energy you wish to project into an environment – whether it be gravitas, authority or just a quiet, relaxed presence.

Exercise: Learning to centre

You may already know how to centre and use this skill when it comes to engaging in sport, the arts or presenting to name a few well-known contexts. If you do have your own approach, you still may find value in the following steps.

Step 1

Become *present*. Bring your awareness to the current 'moment'. If your thoughts are random and dispersed, just focus your attention either on your breathing or on a single object near you (a tree, a flower, a picture, a pen, etc). This is to your *hook* your attention. You are throwing a figurative lasso around your attention, to help you focus and calm your mind. Once you have hooked your attention, you can then direct it.

Step 2

Now that you are present, gently rest one hand on your hara, a few inches below your navel. Begin to breathe into your hara, not in a forceful way, but in a manner that causes your hand to gently rise with the inbreath and fall with the outbreath. To use an analogy, your belly should expand gently like a balloon on the inbreath and deflate gently on the outbreath. Continue this for a few moments till you settle into a comfortable breathing rhythm.

Tip

This can become your signature breathing pattern for any time you want to calm yourself and become present. You can create your own *switch* to just turn this breathing on. Your body will recognise it because what you fire, gets *wired*. Your switch can simply be the thought – *Centre*. Or you just say the word 'centre' to yourself. Your breathing will adjust accordingly, and you will find yourself fully present, resourceful and switched on.

Step 3

NB: This step may be unnecessary, for if you use the previous two steps with discipline, you may find they are all you need to create a state of centredness.

The final step (you can either sit or stand for this stage) requires you to visualise. The example we will use will be a tree. Other examples could be a large bear, a deeply buried rock, or an image of a sitting Buddha, all of which convey a sense of being grounded and connected to the environment you are in.

Select a symbol and feel as if you are that. Either a bear, a sitting Buddha, a rock or a tree or whatever image or symbol works for you. We will choose a tree in this exercise.

As a tree, imagine you have deep roots, penetrating the ground beneath you. This vast root system gives you a profound sense of connection with the Earth and the very ground you stand on. Pause for a moment and just allow yourself to feel that connection with the earth – even if you are on the 14th floor in the Central Business District. (Your mind does not have limitations and can imagine itself anywhere). As you breathe in, feel the oxygen being drawn into your hara, your centre. Hold the breath there for the count of four. Follow this with a relaxed exhalation. After you have exhaled, pause for a moment and then begin the inbreath again and just keep this breathing cycle going for a few rounds. It is important that you feel no effort in the breathing, nothing forced. You should begin to feel a stronger sense of your hara, your centre. And when you feel a strong awareness of your centre, you should feel a strong awareness of your entire self. Sense this pooling of energy and feel it flowing through your limbs to your extremities and to the rest of your body, just as energy radiates from the trunk of a tree through to the extremities.

In a short period of time, you should feel very present, alive, connected with your environment and energised. This is what is meant by 'dynamic stillness'. You are 'still' within yourself; you are not moving physically but your energy is poised and on call and you feel 'centred'.

This process can take minutes or can be initiated in just seconds with practice. When I had to step up and fight in karate tournaments or for gradings, I had only a few brief moments to get centred and bring my best self forward before someone attempted to rearrange me. With intention, it is definitely possible to centre yourself quickly when needed. You may be sitting in your office chair, playing dodgem trolleys in the local supermarket, preparing for the opening bell of a sporting event or about to mount a podium to launch a presentation. Wherever you are, with practise you will be able to centre quickly and effortlessly.

These visualisations, using the image of a tree, bear or Buddha are some that I have used over the years. You may wish to create your own process and select your own symbols. What is important is that you identify a symbol that resonates with you personally and create a process that works.

Tip

When you are distracted by thoughts, or are feeling fearful, or simply discombobulated, breathe it all in. Do not resist such feelings, breathe it in and take it with you. It then just becomes part of your energy field. When you get distracted, or you lose your centre, put your hand back on your hara, and take a few moments to refocus your attention here and breathe into it. If you are in a situation such as the middle of a presentation, or a heated discussion and can't take a few moments out to re-centre, just think – CENTRE – and this will help you refocus.

Those exposed to dangerous work practise similar processes, where a single dedicated word acts as a trigger to generate an immediate response. A similar principle is at play with sirens, flashing lights, or horns which symbolise danger and are intended to force a quick response to a potential threat. When you see a red light at an intersection, you do not have to direct your body's response as the braking happens automatically. Therefore, just saying 'centre' over time, will create the circuitry to assist you to centre quickly. This will become a new, neural shortcut.

This is all fine; however, what happens when the level of fear is so great you cannot centre? Or you try to centre but it does not seem to be effective?

A brief story. Years ago, I had to facilitate a workshop with a group of global leaders for a well-known international consulting firm. These individuals were extremely smart, highly accomplished, top of the feeding chain and had demonstrated little tolerance for those who waste their time. The morning of the first day found me very nervous, far more than I would normally feel at a corporate gig. An added weight on my shoulders was that a good friend of mine, from within the company, had recommended me and I felt an absolute obligation to him to deliver. It was half an hour before our start, and I could feel fear starting to take up residence in both my heart and gut. And this fear was building.

This was powerful energy, not just some minor murmurings, more like a bunch of buffalo playing dodge ball in my belly. I had to address this level of fear with a physical response. Energy wants to move. *Emotion* is from Latin *emovere* which literally translates as 'move out'. Therefore, I had to find a way to allow this energy *out*. I found a quiet place where I would not be disturbed and let the energy move. The sensation was like small waves rippling through my body and whatever energy was present in my throat was expelled using robust exhalations. It worked; the energy moved on. After this somatic release I was left feeling calm and ready to tackle these corporate heavy weights. The session went exceptionally well.

My key learning from this experience was that when fear, or emotional energy is high, a good option is to find some form of safe, physical release. Better this than trying to either ignore it or repress it as you may have seen some hapless souls on podiums attempting to do. I remember well a speaker who was struggling to prevent his hand, and the papers held within it, shaking in a very visible manner. Fear is energy and when it builds it needs an outlet and, in this example, the hand was the point of discharge.

Tip

When you feel fear taking over, and you sense that you have lost your centre, you can get it back quickly according to one of the greatest martial artists of all time, Ueshiba Sensei, the founder of Aikido. In an interview he reflected:

> *'My students think that I never lose my centre. This is not true, I do lose it, but I just get it back quickly.'*
>
> *Master Ueshiba – Founder of Aikido*

I love this quote. To me, it shows his humility, self-knowledge, and similarity to us all. There will always be situations that emerge where we need to be able to self-correct and return to our 'centre'. How frequently do you get knocked off your 'centre' and lose your balance? This could happen at work in the middle of a meeting, when a colleague deliberately emits a loud sigh, or over lunch with a friend, when a comment zips in from left field. You are feeling fine and relaxed one moment, next you are on the defensive. The good news, according to Master Ueshiba, is that you can get your centre back quickly. How? Master Ueshiba would only take a single breath. For the rest of us who are not aikido masters, follow the same principle, breathe into the hara and think 'centre'.

Master Ueshiba's quote is highly relevant in martial arts where, on receiving a hard or unexpected blow, you can be spun right off your centre. If you succumb to the shock, you will fold and be even more vulnerable. If you can regain your centre quickly, you will be back in the game. This is part of the training. This wisdom is applicable in all walks of life for wherever you are, you can lose your way, or be unexpectedly knocked off your balance. Recognise when you lose your centre; don't stay that way ... just act and get it back quickly.

Bring your centre with you

If you have been fortunate to observe a quality Tai Chi practitioner in action, you will see how important balance is in *every* movement. As the leg gently stretches out, the toes connect with the ground, the foot consolidates at this position and then the weight of the upper body is smoothly transferred onto this new position. A moment to pause, centre and then to redirect the flow of energy into the next movement. This is then repeated to the next move and the next one and so on ... Energy being harnessed and consciously directed one moment at a time. There is a poignant symbolism in this practice of *bringing your centre with you*. There is no rush to launch into a new pose, nor an imbalanced redirection of the body hoping to find a stable stance. You are taking your centre with you. What a lesson for life. Centre yourself, identify your next step (related to career, relationship, creative expression, etc.), move out towards it, find a balance point, transfer your centre to this new position, then be mindful of where the next step will be. And then continue this journey into a new aspect of your life, one step at a time, *bringing your centre with you.*

Practising the seamless and fluid movements of tai chi is a wonderful, visceral experience of the flow state. You can read a million words upon the subject, but spend a few moments in a lower horse stance, practising *the tiger returns from the mountain* and you will have a distinct sense of not only what centredness feels like, but also in a broader sweep, the sense of being in flow.

Moving beyond your comfort zone

When you choose to expose yourself to situations of which you are knowingly frightened and you keep repeating this exposure, your brain has a chance to write new scripts. This is called *habituation* as mentioned in chapter 2. Remember the prefrontal cortex and hippocampus can overwrite the amygdala's association with a specific fear or fearful situation.[3] This does not mean a removal of the fear, nor the removal of the trigger that sits in the memory banks within the amygdala, but it provides a new neural pathway that allows for a different and *updated* response. This is critical information for those on a journey towards overcoming, or at least, facing a specific fear. Take yourself out of your comfort zone, engage with the fear with which you have identified and in doing so your brain will get the opportunity to reset its neural wiring.

A brief story to illustrate habituation. One of the key components of learning karate is called *kumite* – which refers to the combat side of the martial arts. Undertaking kumite means having to fight one, or quite frequently, numerous opponents. This was a weekly experience for me in my formative years of karate and initially I didn't look forward to it. I appreciated it was something I had to do but being on the receiving end of numerous broken bones, it was common for me to feel apprehension leading up to kumite. Over time, however, I began to really enjoy it, helped on by allowing my competitive self to surface. The need to match my skills against others became both highly engaging and fun. The fear I initially felt in the lead-up to kumite was just a *short-term* reaction that was replaced by a set of more powerful emotions aligned with being competitive. The constant exposure to this experience of fighting – the habituation I underwent – enabled this emotional transformation. And on occasions, during kumite, I felt in *flow*. These experiences happened when the normal process of conscious decision-making was replaced by an instinctual responsiveness which the speed of combat requires.

Tip

Recognise that fear at times may just be a short-term reaction and not an end point or deal breaker. In situations where you are feeling fear but not in genuine danger, appreciate it for showing up. Embrace it, thank it, breathe it in, centre yourself and then move forward and engage with what is before you, with fear just being part of the 'energy' you are bringing with you. Your capacity to centre yourself will enable you to move beyond what previously had been a fear-based boundary.

Chapter 11: Additional principles and practices from the martial arts

This chapter builds on the practice of centring and introduces some additional principles from martial arts. Why the focus on the martial arts? One reason is because systems such as tai chi, karate and kung fu represent highly visible expressions of the flow state. A sign that a practitioner has achieved mastery is the capacity to demonstrate the flow state at will. When you observe a genuine master in full flight, all the theory to do with the flow state is there before you to see and sense. The other reason, which is more significant, is the fundamental purpose of the martial arts, going back over the centuries, is self-preservation – to help keep the practitioner alive. And because of this need, there exists within the martial arts a treasure trove of practical information, skills and techniques to do with dealing with fear. Self-preservation is the fundamental purpose of the martial arts, and the end game, the ultimate expression, is the state of flow. Utilising the core principles which underpin martial arts will help lead you to a state of flow. With this as context, we will now explore some of the key principles within the martial arts.

Timing

Timing is all about seizing opportunities; opportunities to attack an opponent, execute an effective defence or gain advantage. Opportunities are either seized or created. In the fast world of combat sports, these opportunities may appear in a flash and just as quickly disappear. To be able to capitalise on this, your mind needs to be completely focused, ideally in flow.

This principle is certainly applicable to the wider world. Timing is critical when exciting opportunities arise in areas such as your career, relationships, the corporate world or when you are striving to give wings to creative ideas or adventures. Acting too soon, or too late, comes at a cost. Also consider timing in context to the more mundane aspects of life; when it is appropriate to intervene, when your support is needed or when to show empathy and care. Support arriving too late is just that – too late. Timing is about seizing on moments and making them matter. These moments open briefly and can close in a flash, and they never really come back again in the same way, as the context will shift.

Timing also refers to your capacity to *read a situation* and know if it is the 'right time' to move forward to engage or confront, to step to the side, withdraw or stay still. To be able to do this skilfully requires a sensitivity to the subtle shifts and developments that occur around you. This wise Taoist teaching offers a view on timing, cautioning for the need to attend to things when they are small.

> *'The Sage anticipates things that are difficult while they are easy and does things that would become great while they are small. All difficult things in the world are sure to arise from a previous state in which they are easy and all great things from one when they were small. Therefore, the Sage, while he never*

does what is great, is able on that account, to accomplish the greatest things.' [1]

Tip

Challenges not dealt with sufficiently early tend to get bigger, more problematic and uglier the longer they are left unattended. More people also tend to get invited to the party. When you find these problems on *your* path, as the Taoist wisdom offers, steer towards them and not away, so that you can deal with them whilst they are still manageable.

Balance

Where timing is essential to exploit opportunities, the principle of balance is what enables effective decision-making, the delivery of power and the maintenance of energy.

Currently there exists oceans of information available on 'balance'. And each new tide just keeps bringing more. The macro view relates to how you are in the world – how *balanced* your life is as you navigate through all the difficulties implicit with living in a complex, ever-changing environment capable of throwing curve balls your way – such as a world-wide pandemic, major health problem or rapid reversal of fortune, financially or otherwise.

Balance in this broader view includes how your score card looks in terms of physical, emotional, and psychological factors. I have coached many individuals who have been highly successful in their career, are formidably smart and capable, but have bodies which have really been neglected and appear years older biologically than they are chronologically. Along similar lines, I have often worked with senior, very accomplished corporate leaders who have achieved all that they have set out to do, including amassing great wealth, power and influence. The challenge for many of them is in the final third of their life when they arrive at a certain age and realise that despite all their success, their life lacks a sense of higher purpose or meaning. The area of imbalance for others may show up as a lack of emotional intelligence, deficits in self-awareness, self-regulation, empathy or social skills.

There is no 'ideal' when it comes to assessing balance in a person's life, but it is not too difficult to identify when it is absent. Some individuals are bereft of genuine friendships. Often it is too late, when the realisation sets in that quality relationships have been neglected as other priorities have taken precedence. For others, health, wellbeing and physical fitness is often a low concern until something happens – a revelation of sorts brought on by excessive puffing on a set of stairs, the need to tuck your belly in as well as your shirt, or maybe a call back from the doctor. And for others who have many of the boxes ticked, there may exist a lack of spirituality or a deeper sense of meaning or purpose in their life. A failure to appreciate the quintessential beauty of life and all it has to offer. This frequently results in changes in priorities where contribution to others becomes an enjoyable and purposeful act of service. Others undertake adventures of discovery, questing to connect with their spiritual self or to find a source of inner spiritual nourishment.

So what?

How can you achieve better balance? Can you honestly say you are looking after yourself in terms of overall health and wellbeing? Are you actively building and maintaining quality, loving relationships? If a sense of purpose and meaning is important to you, are you actively pursuing this? When it comes to your work, how can you achieve greater levels of balance? What work can you delegate, where do you need to set stronger boundaries, can you say *No* more frequently to requests for your time and effort?

Where can you be more disciplined and leave work early some days for the gym or for personal or family activities? On this matter alone, it is clearly recognised through extensive research that your brain works better when vigorous exercise is part of your weekly activities. If you have difficulty saying *No* to additional work or find it hard to leave the office at a reasonable time, you need to ask yourself *why*? Invariably fear will be there somewhere – for example, fear of being judged, fear of letting the team down or fear of personal brand damage. In these situations, fear often combines with its other Blues Brother *guilt*, to keep you working longer hours. Whilst you are avoiding the feelings of fear and judgement because of the excessive hours you are clocking on, realise you may instead be laying down resentment. In psychological terms, resentment can be viewed as congealed anger. You don't suddenly feel resentful if someone treads on your toe – this sense of injustice develops over time. As with the example of leaving work early, make sure in trying to avoid fear and guilt you are not laying down resentment. These are not healthy emotions to cultivate.

If the Covid pandemic is requiring you to work from home, what disciplines can you establish to have boundaries around work life and home life? What rituals can you introduce to give you some breathing space from the demands of your computer and mobile? There is a mountain of information out there on this subject. I suggest – keep it simple. Switch the gadgets off at a certain time and keep them off. In this time of respite, exercise, connect with loved ones and find ways to rejuvenate and enjoy yourself.

Tip

With any new habit formation, begin with small steps and slowly reclaim a better sense of balance in your life. This could materialise in a constructive change in how you work, or show up as a new exercise regime or see you pursuing some creative pursuit such as music or art. If you have difficulties reshaping your life to accommodate such affirmative changes, and you justify your inaction with a whole range of *reasonable reasons* as to why not, be careful of your health over the long run. The chances are with prolonged, excessive work, combined with a lack of exercise, and heightened stress a long-term tiredness can kick in, which will impact the quality of your work. I have witnessed this unfortunate occurrence frequently as a coach. The irony is clear; the thing you invested great effort to avoid, such as poor performance or a failure to deliver, arrives at your feet because you are either exhausted or seriously unwell. Find your courage, set your boundaries and begin to create a greater sense of balance in how you operate. These small progressive steps towards greater balance are aspects of life that you have complete control over.

Agility

Timing represents the capacity to seize an opportunity when it arises. Balance enables effective maintenance and leverage of your skills and resources. *Agility* refers to your capacity both physically and mentally to be nimble, able to shift the focus of your attention quickly and effectively. In martial arts, being agile is seen as the capacity to adapt and respond in the moment as required to execute an attack or avoid a threat. Agility captures that sense of fluidity of thought and action. It is the opposite of rigidity where fixed mindsets prevail. Someone who is agile is comfortable in moving off their 'position' when required to, or when better alternatives emerge.

Hence the general is skillful in attack, whose opponent does not know where to defend; and he is skillful in defence whose opponent does not know where to attack.[2]

Sun Tzu

Tip

Applying agility to everyday life requires a willingness to act quickly to seize an opportunity, to move with speed out of a dangerous situation, or to be willing, when needed to adjust your thinking and/or behaviour. When you lack agility in thought and action you potentially become predictable which in some contexts may make you vulnerable.

Distance

How close to the action do you need to be? What is the right distance to keep? In certain circumstances, being too close to the heat could have you crash and burn like Icarus. Too far and you could become irrelevant or marginalised. In karate, distance in combat is always a fluid dynamic. Too far away from your opponent and you cannot have impact; too close for too long and you are vulnerable. Closing the distance, with attention to timing and speed, is crucial. In everyday life it is no different; when to intervene, when to let things be, when to disengage and move on, when to support from the background, when to take a leadership role, when to seize an opportunity?

Distance allows *perspective* and independent *freedom of thought*. Have you seen enough of the bigger picture to make an effective judgement? Are you aware of what agendas are in play? Are you self-aware regarding the type of 'energy' you are bringing with you and the assumptions you have made?

Distance provides perspective and this can be vitally important when it comes to decision-making. To help with maintaining an effective distance, consider the use of the pause button. Something happens. Pause, keep your distance, review your options and reflect upon what course of action to take. Then act. (*N.B. These steps do not relate to situations which require an immediate response*).

Aiki

Aiki-do is a Japanese martial art developed by Morihei Ueshiba as a synthesis of his martial studies, philosophy and spiritual beliefs. Aikido is often translated as, "the Way of unifying (with) life energy" or as "the Way of harmonious spirit". Ueshiba's goal was to create an art that practitioners could use to effectively defend themselves whilst simultaneously protecting their attacker from serious injury.

The word "aikido" is formed from three kanji.

合 – *ai* – joining, harmonising

気 – *ki* – spirit, life energy

道 – *dō* – way, path

The term dō refers to a Way or path, akin to the philosophical concept of Tao. Aiki refers to the principle or tactic of blending with an attacker's movements for the purpose of controlling their actions with minimal effort. One applies aiki by understanding the rhythm and intent of the attacker to find the optimal position and timing to apply a counter-technique. Historically, aiki was mastered for the purpose of killing; however, in *aikido (notice the addition of the 'do')* one seeks to control an aggressor without causing harm. That is the distinguishing aspect of the do. The founder of Aikido declared:

'To control aggression without inflicting injury is the Art of Peace.'

What an intriguing paradox! Learning the martial arts in order to promote peace and harmony and role-model non-aggression.

The aikido approach to dealing with conflict is adaptable to everyday life. In fact, that is the way the founder wanted it. The primary mindset, an inspiring if not novel approach, is to seek to deal effectively with others in conflict situations without causing hurt to anyone involved. When in conflict, or a situation heading in that direction, instead of reacting in a defensive way, the *aiki approach* is to 'blend' in with the 'aggressor' and get their *angle or perspective*. You move to the *centre* of the issue to be able to influence it from there.

In some of the more aggressive styles of martial arts which rely on striking techniques, the approach would be to create distance, notably to defend from a safe position, or to look for an opportunity to attack. This 'blending in' represents a core aikido principle – engage with what energy is present. This *blending with*, applied to life in general, may simply be moving to the point of trouble, hearing from the 'combatants', validating different perspectives and helping all involved to move forward. You are not attacking, taking sides, avoiding, or dispensing blame, but blending with the energy which is present to be able to redirect it in a more constructive direction. At times just being listened to and not necessarily 'agreed' with, can really help quieten down an aggrieved individual.

So what?

The suggestion here is to adopt an aikido mindset when conflict visits you. You do not need to prepare for battle, take sides, run away or launch a pre-emptive attack. Move towards the centre of the issue, listen to perspectives and if possible, redirect the energy. This can be applied to any area of life. An argument around the boardroom table or one around the kitchen table.

A classic exemplar of this *aiki approach* (from the political arena) which has had global significance was the way in which Mikhail Gorbachev steered the USSR during the thawing of the Cold War and the subsequent opening of Eastern Europe. Ronald Reagan received widespread acknowledgement for his role in 1989 when the Berlin Wall came down, but for me, Gorbachev was the real hero. Unlike Reagan, his life was literally on the line because of his courageous, and at the time, radical leadership of the USSR. Like an aikido master he went to the centre and listened to many leaders. His Foreign Minister, Eduard Shevardnadze, cut to the chase and shared his observation that Communism *"was not working"*. He did not push back at the USA, nor Europe, but engaged with his own people, steering them away from conflict and opened the country to perestroika – a major restructure along market principles – and the first steps out of the iron grip of communism. Incredible achievements in hindsight, considering how high and volatile the stakes were and what could have happened at that point in history if the USSR had been led by a more belligerent bully as his recent successors have proven to be.

The aiki approach has a certain symmetry with the Gospel proverb, *'Those who live by the sword, die by the sword'*. Those who propagate violence will in turn be visited by this same energy. A salient reflection for those who default to being bullies at work or in their personal lives. Master Ueshiba, having studied numerous fighting arts in his youth, served in the Russo-Japanese War and witnessed the horrors of World War II including the wide-scale destruction of Japan, knew that the path before him was clear. He was to dedicate his life to teaching aikido as a quest to create a more peaceful world.

According to Ueshiba:

> 'Life is growth. If we stop growing technically and spiritually, we are as good as dead.'

Kime

Fortunately, or otherwise, smashing boards and breaking bricks has helped popularise karate and other martial arts in the Western world. Of these activities, I have done my fair share. I have kicked through bags of tiles and busted numerous boards in moments of unbridled youth. Useful insights did emerge from such practice. To 'break' effectively, you do need *kime* – Japanese for focus. In context to breaking, kime refers to the ability to focus your physical, emotional and mental energy and then direct this force to execute the *break*. If you fail to harness kime and what you are trying to break is substantive, the inert matter will win the day. Broken knuckles, fingers and wrists as well as significant embarrassment frequently results for those who demonstrate such 'breaking' practices in public without kime.

Another insight which surfaced unexpectedly in the practice of breaking, was the moment of *no mind*. Just before you trigger the physical movement to execute the break – i.e., direct the fist towards the board – there is a moment of absolute stillness in the mind. This is difficult to explain, but very real in the experience. Before the execution there is a visceral focus. The mind is active in aligning everything – posture, breath, distance and relaxation to successfully execute the break. But just before the actual break happens, there is a moment of absolute *emptiness* in the mind. A complete stillness. *No mind.*

This is an intriguing juxtaposition of two extremely distinct states.

One moment you are completely still, *no mind*, the next, every part of your being is aligned and forcibly driving a fist or foot, into and through a physical barrier. This change in state happens in a nanosecond. As with my story of the heli sea training in chapter 7, once you are *present* you can change your state in a flash if required.

Activities to do with 'breaking' come with a warning – *don't try this at home* – nor seek to find your own version of enlightenment by breaking through a wheelbarrow full of tiles.

Breaking is commonly used in today's martial art classes as a metaphor for *breaking through* something – a barrier, a limiting belief, low self-esteem, etc. – to get to the *other side*, to a new paradigm. This is an empowering and memorable exercise, particularly for teenagers, who are often dealing with issues to do with self-esteem and confidence. Relating this concept to life, many individuals would be well-served by accessing their *kime* – their inherent and often untapped capacity to focus and direct energy. You do this every day, but you may be unaware of when you are using your kime.

There is value in making the unconscious, conscious. What is meant by this, is that most likely you already use kime and these other martial art principles in your life – timing, balance, agility and aiki – but are unaware when you do. By becoming more aware of them as tools or techniques, you are better positioned to consciously apply them in everyday life. To test this theory, next time you are confronted with conflict, *consciously* choose one or more of these principles to help guide your actions. If you were to choose an aiki approach, move towards the conflict, not away from it, get the perspective of the other and see if you can steer their energy towards a more harmonious position without making them wrong or creating a win/lose outcome.

Reflection

The real benefit in taking up a martial art rests in its vigorous and vital engagement with life and for a genuine student, there are no half measures once you have taken your first footsteps along the 'do'. As previously stated, the word 'do' which is at the end of Budo, Aikido, Kendo, Iaido, Kyudo, Karate-do denotes 'way'. There are many meanings associated with 'do' – such as technique, doctrine, philosophy – but at a deeper level it refers to a spiritual path. The kanji symbol of *'do'* looks like a person on a path. Without the 'do', the fighting arts are essentially just that, sport centred upon combat.

A distinctive quality of the martial arts is the path and guiderails they provide to help transform the behaviours of challenged youth, ranging from the disaffected, the overly aggressive or the withdrawn and introverted. There is something very powerful and unique in the way martial arts provides discipline, creates a safe and purposeful outlet for aggression and invites the shy to find their warrior within. The student who enters a credible school will be first introduced to a strong set of values which promotes non violence and restraint. Their journey will then begin with rigorous and disciplined training and over time they will learn combat techniques and drills which are centuries old. The training will require them to engage with the physical, emotional, psychological and spiritual dimensions, in a unique and dynamic way and give constant opportunity for them to improve their overall wellbeing, confidence, self-awareness and self-esteem.

The martial arts also provide a pathway for those desiring a direction away from a world which appears increasingly superficial, all-consuming and on overdrive. Whether it be tai chi or Thai boxing, once you step into a dojo, you are entering a sanctuary. And over time, the dedicated student will eventually discover that at the heart of traditional martial arts lies a compelling paradox. One studies violent techniques to discover an inner peacefulness; intense, dramatic movement to find stillness; and an overall immersion in the rigours of the physical to find a gateway to the spiritual. And finally, in training in the martial arts, the student is constantly given the opportunity to experience the beauty and aliveness of being in flow.

Chapter 12: Distinctions between Western and Eastern thought

You didn't come into this world. You came out of it, like a wave from the ocean. You are not a stranger here.

Alan Watts

This chapter is focused on providing a high-level perspective on the historical and philosophical context from where the idea, or construct of flow, has emerged. This requires a brief journey into Western and Eastern systems of thought, both of which embody great richness, depth and complexity. These few paragraphs will provide only a mere skim of the surface. Exploring the background of Eastern thought is like sifting through mists. The development of Western thought, however, is more visible and accessible.

The Western view

Western philosophy has its primary origins stemming from the ancient Greeks. This vast and intricate body of wisdom was then expanded upon and enriched by Latin scholars and philosophers during the centuries of

Roman domination. These developments in Western philosophy were in turn, to be heavily influenced by the emergence of Judeo-Christianity. The growing influence of these religions contributed significantly to help shape the ongoing development of Western philosophy, ethics and spirituality in the first millennium.

The second millennium witnessed the emergence of the eminent and increasingly questioning scientists, artists and philosophers who from the Renaissance onwards championed reason, research and logic to challenge the prevailing precepts of the Church. As vibrant and expansive as these times were, they were also very challenging for many educated and thoughtful souls who felt inspired to offer different views on the cosmos beyond the Church's teachings. One clear example of this tenuous situation is reflected in the dilemma the inspired scientist Galileo Galilei found himself in during the early decades of the 17th century. Should he keep promoting his heliocentric view of the cosmos, or reluctantly acknowledge the geocentric teachings of the papacy? Under the threat of being slowly tortured to death, he decided to return his heliocentric thesis of the cosmos to the draft box and get with the Inquisition endorsed, papal program which had the Earth at the centre of the Universe. Galileo was eventually fully pardoned by the Church for his 'indiscretions', though he did have to wait a while. This event took place in 1992.

Despite powerful resistance from the Church, science continued to flourish in the 17th and 18th centuries, culminating in the Age of Reason, otherwise known as the Enlightenment. This vast movement represented a determination to apply critical thinking and reasoning to cultural, religious, social and philosophical matters. Humanity was becoming curious about itself and challenging the influence of a distant, all powerful God and the constrictive dictates of the Church. The 19th century witnessed the expansion of this curiosity from the observed reality to the hidden subconscious realm – an inward journey which saw psychoanalysis gradually gain legitimacy under the commanding authority of Sigmund Freud. The field of study known as psychology also emerged, championed by researchers in both Europe and the United States. This science has continued to expand at an astonishing pace, right up to our current times.

In recent decades, and of critical significance to this guide, psychology has moved away from primarily focussing on our pathologies – what is going wrong with us – to researching that which is within us that will enable us to flourish in the world and enjoy our lives. This is the foundation from which Csikszentmihalyi found his inspiration to initially research happiness and then move on ultimately, to study flow states. To the degree to which flow is a modern construct in the body of contemporary Western philosophy, it is the opposite in the East where flow has its source in antiquity.

The Eastern view

Eastern philosophy, like its Western counterpart, has a very long and rich lineage and is drawn from many sources, including Confucianism, Taoism, Hinduism, Buddhism, Shinto and Zen. Among these many bountiful springs and tributaries which make up Eastern thought, this guide will focus on flow and to do this, we need to start with Lao Tzu.

Lao Tzu was a scholar and philosopher whose final acts in life, according to legend, were to write his masterpiece, the *'Tao Te Ching'* and then ride off into the sunset on a water buffalo. First published around the 3rd Century BC, the *'Tao Te Ching'* contains eighty-one short and highly perplexing verses and has been described as an enigma wrapped in a mystery. These verses are rich with analogy, metaphor and esoteric references which can be challenging for a reader unaccustomed to Eastern thought. If the student has patience however and learns the basic principles underpinning Eastern wisdom, they will be eventually rewarded with profound and piercing insights into the human condition; in particular, nuanced reflections on how to live a life in balance as well as the implications if such guidance is shunned.

Though meagre in volume, these lyrical verses, more than any other text or teacher are responsible for the emergence of the spiritual teachings now known as Taoism – pronounced 'Daoism'. This wisdom has endured over the centuries and is now revered and held in equal esteem with the other great teachings of the East including Buddhism, Hinduism and Zen. Among the many fountains of wisdom within Taoism, the philosophy of flow, or frequently interpreted as *wu wei*, has inspired great interest and reverence throughout the world over many centuries.

Flow. The Western versus Eastern perspective

Though both East and West share common ground when it comes to philosophy, the focus of the following pages is to explore their major points of difference. This includes how *flow is* understood and 'lived' in the East compared to the contemporary Western view. These distinctions include contrasting perspectives on the nature of existence and the role of the individual within it.

Individualism versus the collective

In the West, *individualism* acts as a guiding principle. It promotes independence, self-reliance and freedom of action. As a philosophy which guides thinking and behaving, it is highly valued, championed and protected. Find your own path, forge a way forward, strive to be successful and hopefully you will be rewarded for your efforts. Others may also benefit from the largesse that you have created. On the macro level this can be seen in the promotion and expansion of capitalism. This philosophy of robust self-determinism creates a sharp contrast to the East, which places the *collective* in the position of pre-eminence.

Eastern thinking has as a first principle the primacy of the whole. It does not aspire, like the West, to separate parts from the whole to understand them, but rather it does the opposite. Embrace the whole first to understand the role and purpose of the parts within it. Unity is the beginning and the end.

The linear path versus the circular

In the West, there is a prevailing perspective that the arc of one's life is linear. This is reflected in the Christian doctrine of the soul's journey, where, according to these teachings, you have just one opportunity here, so the loaded suggestion – *live accordingly to what we tell you*. Particularly if you wish to be rewarded in the afterlife. If you don't follow the prescribed path, the downside has not been promoted all that well by the Christian elders – eternal damnation as the starting point. These stark and guilt-inducing views promoted by the Church have been eroded over the centuries, aided by the increasing prominence and reliance upon science. In championing the rational mind, science has in many ways, supplanted religious dogma, with a facts-based narrative reaching into all areas of the human condition. Where science and religion concur is on this linear nature of life. You are born, you live, and you die – seems to be a fair bit of evidence out there to support this contention. This point of alignment between science and religion does not include death. Whereas Western religion teaches of the afterlife, science persistently requests evidence. This impasse is wonderfully captured by the late actor Jimmy Cagney, who in the role of a gangster about to be hung, turned to the priest who was administering the last rights and said;

> *"Well Father, I guess I am going to find out in a few minutes what you guys have been guessing about all your life!"*

Has there been a more salient observation on the mystery of death than this one?

In Eastern philosophy, existence is viewed as circular and for many this includes the belief in the cyclic nature of the soul through the process of reincarnation. As all things are a part of this one Unity, the primary purpose of the individual is to serve and contribute to the collective wellbeing.

Spiritual illumination

In a religious/spiritual context, both the West and the East teach that the ultimate objective in life is spiritual illumination. How this is defined and what paths will lead to it are however viewed quite differently. In Taoist teaching, spiritual development lies in the subjugation of one's identity in an attempt to merge with the great cosmic dance of the Tao. On this path, the ego is suppressed and not encouraged to shine or stand out. A Japanese saying is – *If a nail sticks out, hit it back in*! In the West, if one was to be so pure as to gain enlightenment they would be celebrated, given sainthood and most likely have cathedrals named after them. In the East, if enlightenment is achieved by a dedicated soul, that individual tends to disappear from life, just as Lao Tzu did, riding off into the sunset on his buffalo. This philosophy, which extols humility, virtuous living and service to others, is reflected in this Taoist saying;

Come without fanfare
Work without recognition
Leave without trace

The whole versus the sum of the parts

In the West, to understand how anything works, the usual approach is to break it into its component parts. This may refer to a human body, a galaxy, a mathematical equation, an issue to do with ethics or the functioning of the atom. In contemporary terms this falls under the definition of *reductionism*, defined as;

> *An approach to understanding the nature of complex things by reducing them to the interactions of their parts or to simple or more fundamental things.*

It is difficult to understate the degree to which this methodology has contributed to the advance of our understanding of life and all the things which make it up. There is, however, reason for caution. In reducing things into their component parts, what is often overlooked is how the parts are assigned value and how they are prioritised. The famous axiom *I think therefore I am* voiced by the great seventeenth century French philosopher and scientist Rene Descartes, reflects this Western approach to reducing things to parts and creating hierarchies of importance. This view, proffered by such a prominent individual, contributed significantly to elevating the primacy of the mental faculty and conversely relegating the senses, the emotions and the physical body, to be considered of significantly lesser importance.

It has only been in recent years that science has been able to clearly establish the absolute interconnectivity of the mind and body and highlight the critical role emotions play in guiding us and ensuring overall wellbeing.

This reductionism can be seen in Western medicine which tends to focus primarily on the symptom and not the overall system or the source of the symptom. This contrasts with traditional Oriental medicine where the approach to healing is a systems approach. First assess the overall wellbeing of the patient, in particular their energy level, otherwise known as chi or ki, before attempting to diagnose a specific treatment.

Viewing the world in terms of its 'parts' has contributed to the broadscale ravages against nature. If you don't identify with something as being part of yourself, your clan, tribe, or nation, or you, being part of it, then why assign it value? Why care? Do as you will! And all the better if you have the military, political and financial might to back your cause and drive your agenda. Jacques Cousteau poignantly reflects this dynamic in his statement – *People protect what they love*. In this case he was referring to our need to love our environment, particularly our oceans. What we love, we care for and put effort in to protect. The pervasive attitude among many, that humanity is somehow separate and superior to its surroundings and is entitled to do as it will, has helped unleash unbridled exploitation of the very source which sustains its existence. This failure to identify with the natural world and to protect it has confounded and appalled the indigenous cultures over the centuries who have long recognised how our wellbeing, and that of nature, are one and the same, as are our fates.

As Western thinking breaks things down to understand their origins and function, Eastern thinking starts with the whole. This approach is clearly illustrated in the opening lines of the 'Tao Te Ching'.

> *A way that can be walked*
> *Is not The Way*
> *A name that can be named*
> *Is not The Name*

Putting it simply, the reader is thrown in the deep end. Even the masterful Carl Jung acknowledged being greatly challenged in attempting to penetrate Eastern thought;

> *The great difficulty in interpreting this (Tao Te Ching) and similar texts for the European mind is due to the fact that the Chinese author always starts from the centre of things, from the point we would call his objective or goal; in a word he begins with the ultimate insight he has set out to attain. Thus, the Chinese author begins his work with ideas that demand a most comprehensive understanding on our part.*[1]

As Jung points out, this famous book begins at the epicentre, the Way. An interpretation of this can be the need to live a life in a manner and accord which ultimately leads to spiritual enlightenment. So, from the beginning verse, the reader is met with the ultimate objective – find the '*way*' or personal path to eventually merge with the greater '*Way*'. No introduction, nor sequential build, or scaffolding to help with interpretation, nor explanation of the constructs, the reader is just dropped in at the centre of the cosmos, where the beginning and the end meet, symbolised as the *Way*. An aspiring student will find no real guideposts to follow. Through trials and tribulations, they are required to find the path within themselves. And if at some stage of their studies, they claim to have found it, the *way to the Way*, they would be ridiculed by their teachers. Such proud, egoic articulations would clearly demonstrate that the student has failed to comprehend the real truths veiled within the pathless path.

In comparison, the methodologies used to interrogate reality by such great thinkers from the West as Socrates, Plato and Pythagoras were very different. Reasoning and logic were the foundation of their pedagogy, and dialogue and debate the conduits used to impart knowledge and discern 'truths'. This contrasts with the East, where there is caution regarding reliance on written and spoken language as a means to find higher 'truths'. Since they regard written and verbal communication to be full of constructs, definitions and labels, teachers of Eastern wisdom believe 'language' can hinder the seeker questing deeper meaning and true knowledge. According to the East, this can be attained only through direct, personal experience and cannot be passed on through instruction or books. This direct connection with higher 'realities' or 'truths' is obtained through austere meditation practices such as found in Zen training, in highly disciplined martial arts schools such as the Shaolin, or in returning to and merging with nature as Shinto teaches.

There have been celebrated teachers over the centuries who have acted as bridges between the West and the East. Carl Jung is an outstanding example as is the great Albert Einstein. The latter's thinking, though underpinned and guided by the rigours of science, is incredibly expansive, philosophical and at the same time, deeply compassionate.

> *'A human being is a part of the whole we call the universe, a part limited in time and space. He experiences himself, his thoughts and feelings, as something separated from the rest – a kind of optical illusion of his consciousness. This illusion is a prison for us, restricting us to our personal desires and to affection for only the few nearest to us. Our task must be to free ourselves from this prison by widening our circle of compassion to embrace all living beings and all of nature.'*[2]
>
> *Albert Einstein*

This concise snapshot of the existential challenge we all face links the

Eastern view of the whole – the Universe and everything within it – with the Western focus on the individual's struggle to experience beyond his or her limited and distorted view of this reality.

With this high-level view in place of some of the fundamental differences between Eastern and Western thinking, as well as where they connect, we will now begin our deeper exploration of flow, starting in the West.

Chapter 13:
Flow – the Western view

It's all about where your mind's at ...

Kelly Slater
Eleven times world surfing champion

To experience flow – according to a Western viewpoint – requires you to be able to concentrate your mental or psychic energy. As we have started to explore in previous chapters, heightened levels of fear are a major obstruction to experiencing flow as it causes a fight or flight reaction which absorbs and redirects psychic energy into a survival process. The state of flow is contrary to that of experiencing fear and can be defined as;

> *... a mental state of operation in which a person in an activity is fully immersed in a feeling of energised focus, full involvement, and success in the process of the activity.*[1]

Sports, the arts, hobbies and workplace settings all provide the context for experiencing flow, as do day-to-day activities such as being in nature, engaged with friends and family and expressing oneself creatively. In flow, time seems to be altered, self-consciousness is absent and a sense of full engagement in the moment prevails. Flow can occur anywhere, at any time and it does not have to be dramatic. It can occur whilst you are absorbed in a good book or engaged in a quality conversation.

So, what specifically enables flow to happen?

According to Csikszentmihalyi, flow tends to occur when a *'person's skills are fully involved in overcoming a challenge that is just about manageable.'*

If the gradient of a challenge is too great, relative to one's skill level, anxiety or some form of fear, will emerge. If the challenge is too low, relative to available skills, boredom or apathy will eventually show up. In the first example, flow will not occur as the mind/body attention will be impacted by fear, showing up as excess stress or anxiety. With a challenge too low, there is no need for psychic energy to be focused, nor is there any real challenge, and accordingly, you will not be stretched and flow will not happen. In addition to this, the activity itself needs to be intrinsically appealing. This observation by a classical dancer evocatively captures what happens when flow is experienced.

> *'Your concentration is very complete. Your mind isn't wandering, you are not thinking of something else; you are totally involved in what you are doing ... your energy is flowing very smoothly. You feel relaxed, comfortable and energetic.'* [2]

So how do we get to have similar extraordinary experiences? To answer this, we will start with the Flow Model and explore the mindsets, skills and behaviours required to engender this state.

The Flow Model

This is a simple model[3] though one rich with implication. Particularly if you are involved in some form of leadership. Over the many years of presenting this model, I have noticed how people quickly 'get it' and then move on, without really appreciating the breadth and depth behind the apparent simplicity. If you allow yourself more than just a cursory viewing, the model can provide a lens through which one could contemplate much of life. Career, relationships, creativity and personal development are just some of the dimensions where this model can be effectively applied. In life, in general, how are you showing up? What attitudes or *states* do you most commonly demonstrate; excited, bored, life loving, optimistic, fearful, confident, joyful, resigned, cynical, engaged? Are there crucial areas of your life that you wish to change? The Flow Model can help guide you with this transformation and what is critical to long term success, is a willingness to continually take an *active* position to what life presents you with.

There are two key axes to the model – *skill* level on the horizontal and *challenge* level on the vertical. As we progress along both axes the skill and challenge levels increase respectively. The two major opposing poles are Flow and Apathy. Flow represents full, engaged, enjoyable involvement in a challenging situation. Apathy, a state of being withdrawn, disinterested or disengaged.

Please note: In the paragraphs following, context is important – how one may be in a work environment does not necessarily reflect how one may be in other situations – such as on a sporting field, in family settings or in pursuing a creative expression or hobby.

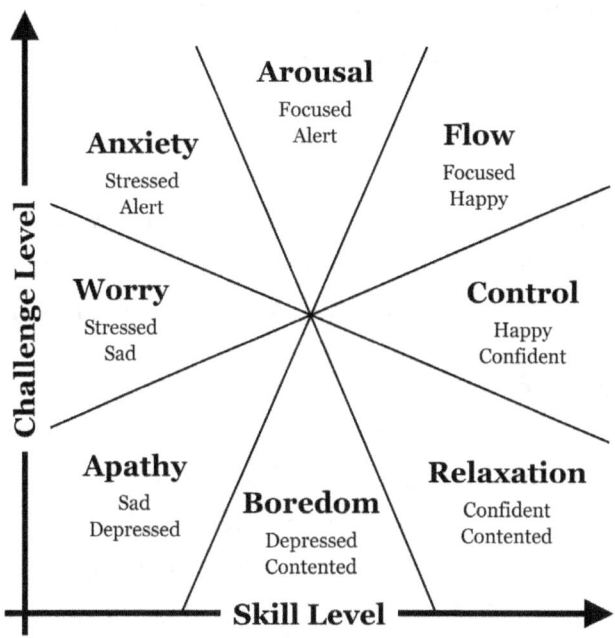

To explain this model, Csikszentmihalyi used a simple analogy of a trainee tennis player. This individual plays at a basic skill level, capable of hitting the ball over the net to an opponent and returning the shot. They feel comfortable with their game and their skill level is commensurate with the challenge faced. If this player continues practising, their skill level will improve. If the challenge does not increase over time however, boredom will set in. To circumvent the arrival of boredom, the challenge needs to be increased. One option is to compete against more experienced players. If this happens there is the possibility of fear or anxiety being sparked, as their current skill level is not equal to this increased challenge. At this point, the player has two key options available to avoid feeling the discomfort of playing a more talented opponent. They could back away and find an easier opponent. Alternatively, they could respond to the challenge and work on improving their skill level to match the higher gradient of their more capable opponent. Though this is a simple example, it illustrates why Csikszentmihalyi saw flow activities as an opportunity for growth.

> *It is the dynamic feature that explains why flow activities lead to growth and discovery. One can not enjoy doing the same thing at the same level for long. We grow either bored or frustrated and then the desire to enjoy ourselves again pushes us to stretch our skills, or to discover new opportunities for using them.*[4]

In the pursuit of flow, there exists this invitation to continually *stretch our skills* and improve in a chosen area or activity. Cameron Smith the Australian Rugby League legend, considered by many to be the greatest player of all time, recently retired at 37. In an interview, fielding questions about his longevity, he responded, that right up to his retirement he still felt motivated, enjoyed his game and recognised that he still had things to learn. Self-motivated individuals, such as Smith, who seek out continual improvement in chosen areas or disciplines are what Csikszentmihalyi calls *autotelic*.

Autotelic qualities

The word 'autotelic' is made of two words with Greek roots. *Auto* meaning self and *telos*, goal. An activity which is autotelic is done for its own sake, for the reward is in the doing.[5] Prestige, remuneration and other external motivating factors are recognised as extrinsic or an exotelic motivation. When this concept is applied to personality, it refers to;

> 'An individual who generally does things for their own sake, rather than in order to achieve some later external goal'.[6]

People who experience flow tend to demonstrate these autotelic traits. They engage deeply in activities and enjoy the experience for its own sake. Autotelic personalities have high levels of intrinsic motivation and are not prone to excesses of fear, self-consciousness or self-centredness. Too much of these traits and the ability to focus psychic energy will be impaired. When fear is not a factor and the mind is clear of distractions, such as self-consciousness or the need to impress, psychic energy can be effectively concentrated and directed.

> 'Autotelic personalities are not necessarily happier, but they are involved in more complex activities and they feel better about themselves as a result. It is not enough to be happy to have an excellent life. The point is to be happy while doing things that stretch our skills, that help us grow and fulfil our potential. This is especially true in the early years. A teenager who finds themselves happy doing nothing is unlikely to grow into a happy adult'.[7]

Reflection

Where in life do you believe your autotelic personality shows up? What are those activities that you love doing, that stretch you and that you find intrinsically rewarding? Do you need to reboot some of these in your life in order to experience more flow? They may have been relinquished as your life experienced more complexity. Or you may just be squandering time, hanging out in your comfort zone, neither excited, nor fearful, just clocking up time giving free reign to the daimon of your unmotivated Self. Reconnecting with your autotelic qualities could be as simple as getting back to nature, returning to a loved hobby or sport, or blowing the dust off the instrument in your cupboard and striking the first note.

The Challenge Axis

As the gradient of challenge increases, relative to the skill level, *Worry* and *Anxiety* are likely to be experienced. Though often unrecognised, it is fear, which drives these states of Worry and Anxiety. This can happen when people are *thrown in the deep end* with the expectation they will hopefully learn to swim. Some do end up swimming and identify the *deep end* as a pivotal learning experience. Many though sink and feel damaged by the process. An alternative to this *sink or swim* scenario is to give people challenging situations where they will be stretched, but they are also given sufficient resources, feedback and encouragement to be successful. 'Stretch' is not referring to volume, a distinction often missed by managers, teachers, leaders and coaches. 'Stretch' refers to learning new skills, being given more challenging opportunities and granted greater autonomy.

Preceding the state of flow is *Arousal*. Arousal represents a state where you are focused, engaged and curious. The skills you have are either commensurate with, or close to, the challenge you are facing. What distinguishes this state from flow is the inability to fully focus psychic energy because fear may be present. This emotion may be brought on by excessive pressure, expectation, or a lack of experience.

The Skill Axis

Tracking the model counterclockwise, this axis contains the states *Apathy, Boredom, Relaxation and Control*. Apathy is self-explanatory – low skills and low challenge can quickly induce this state. Boredom arises once a job or activity is mastered and the challenge is not increased. This is especially evident in work based around repetitive activity. It may have been engaging for a while but eventually people just check out, keeping enough awareness switched on to avoid falling into the machine. As excess worry and stress can result in poor outcomes, so can being underutilised. People frequently leave jobs because they are simply bored or feel they are not developing. This dynamic is captured in the model, where skill levels are high but not matched by the challenge. The state of *Relaxation* may permeate for a while, but if the gradient of the challenge is not dialled up, then boredom will result. This is often seen in the workplace where people who feel they are not being developed eventually vote with their feet. This is an avoidable loss which points to the importance of organisations investing in continuous learning and job rotation. If you are an employer, you would be well-advised to ensure your people are truly engaged for it is the primary driver of performance.

Travelling north of *Relaxation* we meet up with *Control*. This is where the challenge has increased too much to be 'relaxed' and what is needed is a higher level of concentration. Maintaining 'control' requires a lot of energy and focus and the fear of losing it is a prevailing concern. Controlling personalities like to be *'in control'* and are hesitant to surrender or stretch themselves towards flow as this more fluid state may challenge their capacity to remain in control. (*N.B. What is being referred to here is very contextual. A manager at work who is highly controlling, may get to the weekend and let loose and be a total free flowing surfing wizard or a jazz maestro.*)

The Flow State

And finally, we have arrived at the *Flow* state. This is where your capability, though being stretched, is up for the challenge you are confronting... but only just. Therefore, you need to pour yourself into the moment, concentrate your energy and bring the best of you forward.

🎒 Exercise

Reflect on an area in your life where you would like to experience flow (or more flow). Find something you feel passionate about. This could relate to career, a creative expression, sport, hobby, relationships or some other area. We will label this as your objective.

_____
_____
_____

Review the Flow Model. In the context of your flow objective, where would you place yourself currently on the model?

_____
_____
_____

What keeps you at this point and holds you back from experiencing more flow? Is this to do with fear, *needing to be in control, a lack of focus and discipline, over work, a lack of confidence and self-belief or a combination of these elements or other aspects?*

_____
_____
_____

Of the above, which is the most prominent block to you moving closer to flow?

_____
_____
_____

Having identified this, what are your options in terms of reducing this block?

___

Could you begin to improve this situation by creating some new micro habits? If this idea resonates with you, what could those micro habits be?

___

Tip

Take some time to think about these questions. If you do decide on a plan of action, what will be your first steps?

___

The flow state is frequently witnessed in elite sports. There are thousands of moments where athletes have stepped up, found their flow and triumphed in the face of extreme difficulty. Kieren Perkin's gold medal swim in the 1996 Olympics is a fine example of this. He scraped into the final at 8th place and most commentators were writing him off, some in an almost a patronising manner. Kieren had a different perspective. He found the front early and never looked like surrendering it. Though unwell, he just found his rhythm and kept powering on. Courage, tenacity, skill and self-belief all fired together enabling him to secure his second gold medal and in turn, the enduring respect of a nation.

Rock climbing legend Alex Honnold, who featured in the documentary 'Free Solo', is a prime example of what a person can achieve when they reach a state of flow. This film focuses on Alex's death-defying ascent on El Capitan, the 1,000-metre vertical rock formation in Yosemite National Park, in 2017. In just under four hours, he ascended the sheer granite cliff face, climbing without any ropes. He is the first person in history to achieve this feat. One false move, over the four hours, would have resulted in a plunge to certain death. The fine line between living and dying came down to subtle variations on the rock face which allowed him the most limited of hold.

> *"... imagine, like a smooth wall of rock – a nearly vertical granite slab with tiny ripples for your hands and feet. And so, you are really trusting the rubber on your shoes to stick to these ripples."* [8]

I appreciate his capacity for understatement. He was literally relying on that tension created between the rubber of his shoes and slight rises in the otherwise smooth granite, to ensure he did not slip to his death. Many skills are in play at such pivotal moments, but according to Honnold, this did not include his thinking.

> *"I'm not thinking about anything when I'm climbing, which is part of the appeal. I'm focused on executing what's in front of me."* [9]

The purpose of highlighting this rare achievement is to give an extreme example of sustained flow. Individuals often speak about moments of being in the Zone, or in flow. This however was a four-hour, life-on-the-line at every minute, test. His achievement is a profound example of what is possible within the human condition. The real benefit of his achievement lies in its capacity to inspire others to listen to their heart, find their path, focus their energy, train their butts off and ultimately, pursue their dreams with a honed intent.

Another endearing dimension to the flow state is its ability to be transformative. According to Csikszentmihalyi, within the flow experience the individual can be elevated beyond where they had been previously and, in the process, have their confidence, capability and self-belief strengthened.

> *In our studies, we found that every flow activity, whether it involved competition, chance, or any other dimension of experience, had this in common. It provided a sense of discovery, a creative feeling of transporting the person into a new reality. It pushed the person to higher levels of performance and led to previously undreamed-of states of consciousness. In short, it transformed the self by making it more complex. In the growth of the self lies the key to flow activities.*[10]

Csikszentmihalyi's choice of the verb *transformed* is no accident – it is a potent word. One which is often incorrectly used as a synonym for *change*. Transformation speaks of something more profound. When *change* takes place, one can always revert to a previous state. A smoker, who drops the habit, can over time *change* back to smoking. Transformation is a different quality. If something is transformed, such as a butterfly from a chrysalis, the previous state cannot be returned to. The state has been transformed. Therefore, when you experience flow, it transforms you, you can't go fully back to a previous state, an earlier way of being or a former attitude. You have had a glimpse into what is possible within your own bounds of experience and once having enjoyed flow, a new benchmark is set.

I am certain Alex Honnold would have found his ascent of El Capitan transformative. In interviews after his astounding feat, he frequently refers to the moments of perfection he felt;

There is a satisfaction to challenging yourself and doing something well. That feeling is heightened when you are for sure facing death. If you're seeking perfection, free soloing is as close as you can get. And it does feel good, to feel perfect, for a brief moment.[11]

And just in case you are not the kind of punter to hang off a thousand-metre rock face, with nothing but a few sweaty fingerholds and half an inch of rubber to keep you from separating from your mortal coil, outlined below are some practical and less life-threatening ways on how you can find flow in your everyday life. For what Csikszentmihalyi discovered in his research was that though the conditions for flow can just spontaneously emerge, we can also actively set them up.

Setting up the conditions to experience flow

When the term flow is used colloquially it is often in reference to *going with the flow*, merging in with what is happening, not resisting the direction energy is taking. My wave riding story from Chapter One is a prime example of this. The wave and I met at a point and I had the delight of riding it. I did not set up the conditions for this to occur, the ocean did that. I went with the opportunity before me. Though conditions do arise, often unexpectedly, that enable flow, you can consciously create these conditions and not be reliant upon some random synchronicity of events.

Flow is an end state that results as a convergence of a number of conditions. While these conditions often seem to just emerge, we can also organise our environment to maximise the probability that flow will occur.[12]

The following are the conditions which Csikszentmihalyi identified to be the most favourable to enable flow. If you lead, coach or mentor people in some form you may benefit from drawing upon the guidance in this research. Worth noting; not all of these conditions need to be present for individuals to experience flow.

1. **Clarity about outcome**. Having clear goals/outcomes and expectations/rules that are discernible.

2. **The ability to concentrate and focus**. The opportunity is set up so that full attention can be given to a specific area or activity.

3. **Direct and immediate feedback**. Successes and failures throughout the activity are apparent so that behaviour can be adjusted as required.

4. **Balance between ability level and challenge**. The activity is neither too easy, nor too difficult.

5. Having a **sense of personal control** over the situation or activity.

6. **The activity is intrinsically rewarding** so there is an effortlessness of action.

What is assuring is that you can establish these conditions whether you are running a business, following a creative pursuit, being an athlete or otherwise. They are not overly complex or demanding, nor do they require a lot of attention to set up and maintain. How these conditions are interpreted and applied is contingent upon the context. If you are skiing, it is the quality of the snow and the contours of the slope which will be giving you the immediate feedback as required in condition number three.

When goals are clear, feedback relevant and challenges and skills are in balance, attention becomes ordered and fully invested. Because of the total demand on psychic energy, a person in flow is completely focused. There is no space in consciousness for distracting thoughts, irrelevant feelings. Self-consciousness disappears.[13]

This is why flow can be such an elusive experience for many as they get distracted by wayward thoughts, moments of self-criticism, self-consciousness or they feel the need to impress. When these things happen there is an immediate impediment to the concentration of psychic energy necessary to engender flow. Flow will not happen. This underscores the importance of being able to self-regulate and control your conscious mind to experience flow. Being self-aware, learning to centre, embracing your fears and quietening the inner critic are all helpful actions to take in order to set yourself up to experience flow.

🧰 *Toolbox: Questions to help you achieve flow*

Now for some practical steps. The questions that follow align to the 'conditions' covered in the previous two pages and are intended to help you achieve flow. The word 'lead' is mentioned on numerous occasions. 'Lead' here refers to roles such as managers, coaches, teachers, captains, parents and anyone who is in an actual leadership role. 'Pursuit' refers to any endeavour you are investing substantive energy and time into such as a career, business, sport, adventure, hobby or artistic expression.

- How clear are the goals or objectives that either I have personally set, or others have set for me?

- What can I do to ensure I create the conditions to be able to concentrate? Or if I lead others, how can I help them be able to concentrate?

- Can I ask my manager, coach, colleague or mentor for; feedback, or request an increase in the amount of feedback, or the frequency I receive it? Or is the challenge more about the quality of feedback I am receiving?

- If leading others, how frequent and effective is my feedback?

- If I feel I am under-utilised in terms of my skill level and ability, what options can I exercise, or actions can I take?

- Should I apply for other positions, or seek a career path elsewhere?

- Are there further actions I need to take to enhance my options?

- How much autonomy do I have in this particular career path/role/pursuit?

- Do I feel restricted? If so, what are my options?

- Is this career/position/pursuit developing me?

- Do I still feel passionate about this career path, sport, hobby, etc?

- Is there another path for me which will excite my passion and enable me to express myself more fully? If so, what is it, and what steps do I need to take to bring this closer?

A suggestion is to take some quality time out to reflect on these questions. Though they are straightforward, they carry weighty implications.

Enjoyment versus pleasure

The topic of happiness is often associated with flow. According to Csikszentmihalyi, we should not pursue happiness as an end, more as a by-product of doing something which we innately enjoy and that which holds an implicit sense of purpose and meaning. An article[14] he co-authored on positive psychology with Martin Seligman draws the distinction between positive experiences which give pleasure compared to those where the experience is enjoyment. Pleasure is defined in this context as; *'the good feeling that comes from satisfying homeostatic needs such as hunger, sex and bodily comfort'*. Enjoyment refers to; *'the good feelings people experience when they break through the limits of homeostasis – where they do something that stretches them beyond where they were – in an athletic event, an artistic performance, a good deed, a stimulating conversation.'* According to the authors it is *'enjoyment rather than pleasure'*, which leads to *'personal growth and long-term happiness'*. This is an important perspective as many people vainly pursue pleasure as a means to find happiness and fulfilment. A simple example is given in the article where someone would prefer to watch TV and drop into some *'mild dysphoria'* instead of reading a book which may act to both challenge their intellect and nourish their spirit. This example, of course, can be expanded into a much larger context and what becomes clearer is how much of our life is invested in seeking pleasure as opposed to enjoyment.

What has this got to do with flow? By shifting away from the pursuit of pleasure and moving to activities where you experience enjoyment, you are helping create the conditions for experiencing flow, i.e., activities which are intrinsically rewarding. Do a review on how your life is tracking relative to these paradigms. If enjoyment is on the downside of the ledger, then maybe it's time to inflate the tyres on your mountain bike, take the chess set out of the cupboard or even ring that long-lost friend from whom you have drifted.

The Perfectionist

The following 'case study' demonstrates how the flow model can be applied to the professional world. The content, though created by me, is drawn from experiences I have had in actual coaching. The comments here are genuinely representative of countless conversations I have experienced with professionals struggling with the self-generated pitfalls of being a 'perfectionist'. Many of the talented people with whom I have had the pleasure to work with would fall under the definition of being either a perfectionist or its close cousin, the 'anxious over-achiever'. You may see something of yourself in these responses.

Where on the Flow diagram would you spend most of your time?

Between anxiety and worry.

Why these states – what do you identify with?

I often find myself feeling a low grade of anxiety. I tend to worry a lot, mainly about how things could go wrong. I know I am a perfectionist and will often accept other's work, even though it is not up to my standard, and I often redo it myself. This reworking frequently adds extra hours to my normal work and causes frequent late nights. I am aware of this pattern but have not had much success trying to break out of it. I think the worry has also affected my sleeping because I frequently wake during the night and have trouble going back to sleep. This compounds the problem as I am tired the next day and this impacts the quality of what I do and the energy I bring to my team.

What would you need to do differently to get to experience more flow? What behaviours and actions would you need to change?

I think I need to take small steps. Some of these steps could be to trust my team more and delegate more frequently. Also, I am too quick to say 'Yes' to people when they are requesting help. I need to be able to pause and consider my options before agreeing to additional work or accepting sub-standard work from my team. I could also stop being so hard on myself. I am my own worst critic. I heard this line once regarding perfectionism which I think is highly relevant – 'it is an opinion, not a standard'. I do need to change my thinking around this subject. I also need to shift my focus to coaching my team more so that they can step up and cover more of what I am doing.

How would you need to think differently? What mindsets would you need to change?

My thinking needs to change more towards what I am doing right, rather than what I could have done better. With the volume of work coming my way, I just can't keep trying to cover it all myself as well as doing it to the highest standard. My thinking also needs to be more around what really is critical and what are the 'nice-to-haves' and get clear about those distinctions. I have to need to feel comfortable making that call and saying 'No' to some people – I just need to ensure I do this in a constructive way.

Also, I have to let go of needing people's approval ... I am just so invested in people liking me it is limiting my ability to make the right calls. I am aware of this ... I just have to put it into action.

What factors of which you are in control of, hold you back? In relation to these factors, what can you do differently to experience more flow?

Beyond what I have already said, I know I need to plan my time way more effectively. I tend to go around fighting fires and am drawn from one problem to the next. With better planning, I can allocate my team and the resources we have more effectively. This will provide me with greater levels of focus and with this in place, then I feel I can move closer to a flow state. I just want to get back to experiencing enjoyment in my work. I feel for too long it has been more about just enduring.

Sound familiar? Or at least parts of it? If so, what are your options? Where do you need to reshape how you operate? If perfectionism is a key driver for you, it can be very demanding, exhausting and ultimately drain the life force from you.

Tip

When it comes to making changes, start small. Select one area and focus on bringing about improvement. As we have learned in creating new constructive habits, start small, but be consistent. And when you start to notice improvement in this area, recognise it and reward yourself in some way.

So what?

I have seen firsthand, on countless occasions, the upside as well as the downside of perfectionism (or anxious overachieving) in the workplace. The upside is clear. It is the consistent and timely delivery of a high volume of quality work. Career progress and remuneration are the usual rewards for such performance. The downside is equally clear. To deliver such quality performance in a sustained manner invariably causes significant and consistent stress on the individuals. This stress does not just show up in the workplace, but in private lives where health, relationships and overall wellbeing suffer. As explored in earlier chapters, our systems are fine with stress in short bursts, but we are not designed to effectively manage sustained stress loads. Something will pay the price and it is usually to do with health. However, it doesn't have to be like this. Often in the case of perfectionism it relates to a fear of getting it wrong, being judged, found out or found wanting. The cycle is reinforcing as such individuals have to keep proving to themselves and others that they are good and worthy. This is a great result for organisations that benefit from such dedication, but at what cost to the individual? If this is your pattern, please review some of the exercises we have already explored around Mindfulness, Reframing and Centredness. One thing for certain, the mental models that come with such high drive for perfection will prevent the individual experiencing flow. The amount of psychic energy involved in *having* to achieve such high standards deprives the individual of a sense of inner freedom and the ability to surrender into, and be absorbed by, whatever they are doing.

Our focus now shifts to the Eastern view of flow. Though there are bridging points between Csikszentmihalyi's work and the East – particularly around the value of focus and discipline – the Western perspective tends to isolate flow states to certain experiences or endeavours. In the East, flow represents a way to live life.

Chapter 14:
Flow – the Eastern view

To see a World in a Grain of Sand.
And Heaven in a Wild Flower
Hold Infinity in the palm of your hand
And Eternity in an hour

William Blake

To understand flow, or wu wei as it is known in the East, requires an appreciation of the broader stream of Taoism. And what may help with this is to simply pause occasionally and reflect on the greater cosmos including your existence and what purpose your life is serving. As Lao Tzu must have done centuries before, elevate your thinking to embrace the grand sweep of the cosmos that plays out through eternity and awaits you at your doorstep. Observe life unfolding around you, and your part in this. Observe your interconnection with nature and its vital elements – fire (the sun), air, water and earth. Reflect on the fecundity and scale of nature; the oceans and mountains, rivers, ice flows and deserts, fertile valleys, of winds, of waves, of mighty global currents of air and water, great fires, hurricanes and floods, of animals, birds, fish and insects in incomprehensible numbers and variety and the ever-changing splendour of the seasons – and this magnificent opus, playing out through eternity on this small, lonely planet. And then consider earth itself, being but an insignificant dot of matter in an endless, timeless, infinite universe. And on earth, human existence being but a blink of an eye. It is this majestic celestial symphony, with its great structure and order that the Taoist masters have turned to for guidance and inspiration in how to live a life in balance, harmony and in accord with universal laws. And the most visible and immediate expression of this order, is the nature which surrounds us.

> *One who lives in accordance with nature*
> *Does not go against the way of things*
>
> *Verse 8, Tao Te Ching*

So, what is it? What is the Tao? What is this enigma wrapped in a mystery?

A definition by the scholar Dwight Goddard refers to this mystical force as being;

> *A universal creative principle which forms and conditions everything – an intangible, cosmic intelligence which harmonises all things and brings them to fruition.*

Sound familiar? Wisdom from a long, long time ago, born out of a Hollywood film studio. Yes ...! Highly reminiscent of George Lucas's ... The Force. There are however many other fans, from a multitude of backgrounds, attracted to the Tao.

> *Western missionaries found counterparts to God and creation myths; modern particle physicists have found, in Taoism's stunning naturalistic vision, deep insights into relativity and*

quantum mechanics and science-fiction enthusiasts have found 'the Force' of Star Wars.[1]

The title, 'Tao Te Ching', can be interpreted to mean the 'Way of Virtues', though many would disagree with this description. (You know you are in for trouble when scholars can't even agree on the meaning of a book's title, let alone what is contained in the text). At the heart of this philosophy is the central teaching that the universe has an overriding order, balance and purpose to it and as individuals, who belong to this great cosmos, we are advised to discern this order and to live in accordance with it. There are no injunctions as to how one should or must live, such as you would find in Western religious practice, but observations regarding the benefits to be obtained by living according to the Tao or the Way. You are living a life which aligns with and reflects natural laws of harmony and balance or you are not. There is no judgement, nor guilt trips, nor punishments meted out by a displeased God, but the verses do indicate that in failing to heed natural laws, or to be sensitive to the interplay between cause and effect, consequence, or karma, will ensue.

This wisdom in the 'Tao Te Ching' is as relevant today as it was in antiquity. The verses are replete with timeless and universal themes including strategy, leadership, relationships, politics, social order, ethics, virtues and values, metaphysics, life, death and meaning. The book follows no sequential path, nor storyline, but is made up of sharp and poignant observations on both the strengths and vulnerabilities within the human condition. This lack of structure contributes to the delight in reading it. You can open any page, on any verse and be struck by the wisdom present – though it may take a little of your left-of-field thinking to discern the poignant and precious offerings before you.

A few examples of these verses follow which clearly demonstrate the

Taoist way of conveying wisdom through simple observation. Though penned centuries before, they still hold a compelling relevance. As the two current superpowers in the world, the United States and China, increasingly move towards a new Cold War, leaders in both countries could benefit by the simple, yet profound wisdom in Verse 46. This deals with the implications of a state's failure to recognise a drift towards conflict.

When the Tao is present in the empire
men follow their own nature
and riding horses work the fields
When the Tao is absent from the empire
men go astray
and war horses breed on sacred ground

The power is in the simplicity of the message – it cuts through. There are no 'shoulds' or 'musts', just observations. Heed it or not, there will always be consequences when balance is disrupted and harmony disturbed through overreach, greed or the misuse of power. These natural laws of cause and effect abide regardless of whether you are a humble worker or an Emperor.

In verse 66, Lao Tzu has some pointed observations to share about leadership. His following words could be well-heeded by our current crop of world leaders, many of whom are focused on expanding and entrenching their power and ruling as autocrats.

Why do the hundred rivers
turn and rush towards the sea?
Because it naturally stays below them

He who wishes to rule over the people

must speak as if below them
He who wishes to lead the people
must walk behind them
So, the Sage rules over the people
but he does not weigh them down
He leads the people
but he does not block their way

The Sage stays low
so the world never tires of exalting him
He remains a servant
so the world never tires of making him its king

The world has a distinct need for more inspiring, *servant* leaders as there appears no lack of the arrogant, bullying kind. Their suffering people, if not the world, seem to have grown 'tired' of the self-serving ways of some of these dictators, many who have held power for decades. As Lao Tzu indicates, there will be always karmic consequences of overreach and exerting excessive control over others. When it comes to dictators, history clearly shows very few of them get to enjoy a pleasant and restful retirement. Hitler, Mussolini, Tojo, Stalin, Ceausescu, Saddam Hussein, Gaddafi and Charles Taylor are just some examples of leaders who achieved vast power in their life, through brutal and oppressive means, but didn't manage to swan around in their twilight years and enjoy their Super. Putin no doubt will prove to be an interesting case study.

Taoism and the *Way* of water

Lao Tzu counsels those in power to emulate nature, in particular water, for it finds the lowest, most 'humble' point from which to serve, support and nourish. This admiration for water is clear in verse 8.

> *The supreme good is like water, Which nourishes all things without trying to It flows to the low places, loathed by all men*

You may know people who have natures that reflect the best qualities of water. They are generous and caring, are highly supportive of others and they tend to avoid the limelight. They are the opposite of the self-serving egotists who often create the most 'noise' and attract most of the attention. They are enablers, helping creativity to flourish and when in family environments or teams they usually represent the heartbeat. They create a sense of safety and others tend to be drawn to their warmth and gentleness. Like water, they replenish and nourish the people and things which are around them.

Water follows and fulfils its intrinsic nature, and in doing so, all things which meet it, benefit. Even mighty storms and floods are ultimately cleansing and allow for a renewal. This appreciation of water and of nature in general has admirers in the West as well. In reading this verse from the William Wordsworth poem, *Lines written a few miles above Tintern Abbey,* the Tao seems to flow and ebb in every line.

> *For I have learned to look on nature ...*
> *And I have felt a presence that disturbs me with joy*
> *Of elevated thoughts; a sense sublime*
> *Of something far more deeply interfused,*
> *Whose dwelling is the light of the setting suns,*
> *And the round ocean and the living air*
> *And the blue sky, and in the mind of man;*
> *A motion, a spirit, that impels*
> *All thinking things, all objects of all thought,*
> *And rolls through all things.*

I would like to think that Lao Tzu would have been moved by

Wordsworth's poetry, in particular, the very Taoist perception of *'something'* which carries and *'rolls through all things'*.

The following lines by an Inuit Shaman named Uvavnuk also reflect the Tao and in particular, veneration of water.

> *The great sea*
> *Has sent me adrift*
> *It moves me*
> *As the weed in a great river*
> *Earth and the great weather*
> *Move me*
> *Have carried me away*
> *And move my inward parts with joy.*

As evident in these sections of poetry, be it in the West or the East, from antiquity to the current years, the admiration for water is ubiquitous. Expressed and celebrated though all manner of creative arts, this revered element serves as a universal symbol of life and of the lifeforce, of our emotional nature as well as the quintessential expression of flow. What has intrigued its admirers over the centuries is how it contains such strength even though in essence, it is essentially soft, attracting such adjectives as 'weak'. In verse 78, Lao Tzu observes;

> *'There is nothing in the world more soft and weak than water, and yet for attacking things that are firm and strong there is nothing that can take precedence over it.'*

The famous General and strategist Sun Tzu also has a high respect for the intrinsic qualities of water and applied them to tactics in warfare;

> *Military formations are like water. The form of water is to avoid*

the high and go to the low, the form of a military force is to avoid the full and attack the empty; the flow of water is determined by the earth, the victory of a military force is determined by the opponent. So, a military force has no constant formation, water has no constant shape; the ability to gain victory by changing and adapting to the opponent is called genius.[2]

The following section will build on Sun Tzu's wisdom and will broaden our exploration of wu wei (flow) and how it can be applied in a practical context to everyday life.

Principles associated with the Eastern view of Flow

Nature goes her own way, and all that to us seems an exception is really according to order.

J.W. van Goethe

Finding the path of least resistance – Wu Wei

In life, according to Taoist wisdom, there is virtue in pursuing paths of least resistance, just as water does. Whether it be a gentle trickle down a windowpane or the awesome spectacle of a charging river, water follows a course which will minimise energy loss and enable momentum. On meeting obstacles, it either flows around them, wears them down, or patiently builds energy till they can be overflown.

Reflecting on the normal rhythm of your daily life, how frequently do you seek out and select *the path of least resistance*; a choice or a direction where you are most likely to experience an ease of passage? How conscious are you, that with some awareness you might discover easier ways of attending to the challenges that life throws your way?

Or, on meeting resistance in some form, are you more likely to drop your head, bulldoze your way forward, taking no prisoners as you storm the challenge before you?

So what?

There is value in being sensitive to situations in life when taking the path of least resistance is the better option. In selecting such a path, opportunities will reveal themselves, energy will be conserved and the environment you are in will not be overly disturbed. Flowing water naturally shifts shape and responds to the environment as opposed to trying to impose itself on what is before it.

There are exceptions of course, such as tsunamis. They don't need to build their energy; once released, the momentum is already there. They still flow however in accordance with the landscape before them. In watching footage of the devastating effects that the tsunami unleashed on Japan in 2011, it was evident that despite how powerful that vast body of raging water was, it was still following the contours of the landscape before it. In doing this it was conserving energy and expressing its implicit nature – finding and flowing into the path of least resistance.

How do you apply this 'taking the path of least resistance' or wu wei to everyday life, which is fast, complex, ever demanding and constantly changing? We will start this exploration with a fine, instructive sonnet by Shakespeare.

> *There is a tide in the affairs of men,*
> *Which taken at the flood, leads onto fortune*
> *Omitted, all voyage of their life*
> *Is bound in shallows, and in miseries*
> *On such a full sea are we now afloat*

And we must take the current when it serves
Or lose our ventures

> William Shakespeare – Julius Caesar Act 4, Scene 3

A *tide* taken at full *flood*, where the water's depth is at its highest and the current at its strongest, is a wonderful metaphor for wu wei. Applied to life, when situations align so positively, there is wisdom in going with the *flow* before you.

The essential principles of wu wei

The essence of wu wei is challenging to convey in language, something akin to grappling with Zen. In various definitions, it can be interpreted as being *actionless action, effortless action* or what I prefer; '*action that does not involve struggle or excessive effort*'. In avoiding struggle, you are more likely to be sensitive to, and aligned with, the *flow of* life happening around you. Instead of imposing yourself on your environment you attune to the 'currents' which are prevalent in your life. This sounds very esoteric and therefore, the question arises – What does wu wei mean in practical terms of living life?

To answer this question, we will start with what it isn't. Firstly, wu wei is not an encouragement, reminiscent of the 60's, to 'check out' of the mainstream, head to Byron Bay and *just go with the flow* and allow taxpayers to fund your personal quest for enlightenment. This philosophy also does not encourage you to sit in a lotus position and meditate your life away. Wu wei is not about doing nothing or taking no action. When it comes to *action*, wu wei does entreat a sense of doing what is right or virtuous and avoid that which is not. The central idea is to do with not *forcing*. As Alan Watts, the great English philosopher muses, wu wei lies in recognising the *currents*, or *tides* which are present in your life and allowing yourself to be guided by them. He builds further on this analogy by using another analogy, and postulates that wu wei is *"about sailing, not rowing"*. What direction is the wind currently blowing in your life and can you use this energy to propel you forward? Or do you need to rest in a backwater for the winds and tide to change? Sailing into a fierce wind or pushing against a current takes a lot of energy and both are contrary in principle to wu wei which seeks to conserve energy.

Wu wei counsels against being overly attached to rigid forms of thinking or holding too strongly to fixed ideas, beliefs or positions. A river in flow does not hold to a position. How frequently have you sought to 'win' an argument or defend an idea or hold to a position, and after much heated debate and gnashing of teeth, you are left with not much more than a feeling of tiredness and a few embers of self-righteous fervour. Learn to surrender a position when necessary. Wu wei is not about avoiding conflict, but it does promote the wisdom in finding ways to get things done in a manner which conserves energy – just as flowing water seeks to minimise friction and build momentum. When genuine opportunities open for you, something which is aligned to your hopes and ambitions, do not allow fears, self-doubt or apprehension obstruct you. Do not get in your own way! Move towards the opening and allow the flow of events take you with it. Otherwise, you may end up treading water or overstaying where you are.

Once you have decided to move on from something – a career, a company, team or position – do so when the energy is positive and buoyant. This energy will serve you well, like a current or a full tide, to move you to your next opportunity. I have witnessed on many occasions individuals who having overstayed their time in a position, succumb to resentment, resignation and self-righteousness. This usually is then shared to all those around, spreading like a toxic cloud. If the opportunity arises to leave when the energy is good, take it. Otherwise, what may have been wu wei, or *flow*, will eventually turn into a stagnant backwater with no clear direction or momentum to help you find a way out.

So what?

I believe wu wei, or effortless action, refers to appreciating the situation(s) you find yourself in and being able to intuit a way to act which is not about imposing yourself on the situation, but more about flowing or 'sailing' with the flow of events which is happening around you. Wu wei is about how conscious you are regarding the context in which you find yourself, the timing you are choosing to act, your intent and the quality and level of energy you are demonstrating. Forcing an action, which is either poorly-timed, overly self-serving, or not really thought through, can generate significant and painful consequences. Like water, are there areas in your life that you need to pull back from, so you can conserve and build your energy before moving forward? Are you overstretched and are your resources drying up? Are there areas in your life where you need to yield or find another way? Have you been stuck too long in a certain situation, relationship or career and are in more stagnation than flow? Do you need to tap into your courage, place fear into the back seat of your life and find a way to flow beyond this current impasse?

Tip: How to bring wu wei into your everyday life

The philosophy of wu wei may appear a bit idyllic and impractical for this complex and challenging world we live in. It is exactly however for these reasons that you would benefit from the application of this philosophy. Consider the following.

Be kind to yourself – this should be not too hard. Find ways to celebrate who you are. If you are full of self-criticism, consider flipping this. I am sure a tiger walking down a jungle path is not listening to her inner critic. Why is being kind to yourself wu wei? Because it is about conserving energy and nurturing inner harmony. A constant flow of negative thoughts and judgements about yourself and the world generates biochemistry which will reduce your ability to find an inner calm and balance. Find ways to boost your serotonin levels and reduce adrenaline.

Building on kindness, find ways to love and respect yourself. Why is this wu wei? Because it is about creating an inner sense of harmony, peacefulness and acceptance. When you have these qualities as your centre, you don't need to impress yourself upon the external world. You don't need to seek approval from others, nor do you need to prove yourself to anyone. These destructive patterns usually run over decades and require a huge expenditure of energy. When you walk away from such patterns and replace them with a healthy level of self-acceptance, centredness and calm, you have found the doorway to wu wei.

Walk away from some arguments. You don't always need to win them, nor even engage in them. They are often exhausting and can take a toll by taking up residence in your psyche for a surprisingly long time. If you sense an argument building, one which is unnecessary, find a way to dissipate it or redirect the energy.

Be sensitive to openings and opportunities. When they appear and are aligned to your plans or goals, be like water and flow into them.

If you are stuck in some self-destructive pattern or caught up in a situation which is really draining, have the courage to move away. If you stay, you will be building layers of resentment. If you go, you may feel some variation of guilt or fear for a short while. With some self-care these negative feelings will pass. If you stay and the resentment keeps building, it will most likely come at a cost to your health. Putting it simply, being 'stuck' and failing to engage an action to become unstuck, is contrary to flow.

Additional practises and principles aligned with wu wei

Seek for softness

Softness from the Eastern perspective does not equate to a vulnerability or lack of strength or resolve. The apparent softness implicit in gentle moves of tai chi is a good example of this. Those fortunate enough to have trained with a skilled exponent of the art can testify to the incredible power that the gentle, flowing movements of tai chi generate. Here the principle of softness, of yielding and flowing is not representative of a weakness, but of a way to harness and focus power. On my personal journey with martial arts, it took me a long time to appreciate the importance of softness. In my earlier years of training, the harder I tried to extract power from my body, the slower, more rigid and armoured I became. I even used to hit large, hardwood trees with bare knuckles as part of my training. I am sure it provided some comic relief for the trees. As I have learnt to consciously relax at will, speed has increased and with that, power and impact.

As I have aged, it is flexibility which is now most important. Lean on a rigid stick and it will break. A flexible one will yield as it supports you. How flexible and responsive is your body? Medical professionals believe they can assess your biological age by the suppleness of your spine. A Chinese proverb asserts: You are as old as your spine. If the vibrancy of life is best represented by suppleness and high levels of energy, how well are you tracking? If not very well, what are your options? You probably have plenty of opportunities right where you live? Yoga, pilates, martial arts, dance, swimming and walking are all high-quality pursuits capable of reinvigorating both body and mind and helping with flexibility.

So what?

If you are tense, holding on and armouring up to meet life, a significant amount of energy is bound up in that position and, over time, it is tiring and potentially damaging. The negative health implications of exposure to long- term stress have been highlighted in previous chapters. By relaxing, calming the mind and improving your suppleness, energy which may be tightly-coiled inside you can be released. You probably have had this sensation of 'release' following a yoga or pilates class. With a more supple body, your energy will flow better and you will enjoy an increase in aliveness.

'Softness' refers to an ability to adapt and adjust to situations as they arise. 'Hardness' does not have this capacity. To draw upon an old and wise story, as wind moves against bamboo, the bamboo yields. The stronger the wind, the stronger the yielding, and eventually, as the wind tapers off, the bamboo springs back to its original position and continues to thrive. The oak tree however, though deeply-rooted and very strong, is unable to yield to any great degree and will eventually meet a wind strong enough to uproot it. There are times when 'holding' your position is not a wise decision. Likewise, yielding when appropriate is not a weakness.

'The art of life lies in a constant readjustment to our surroundings.'

Kakuzo Okakura

Mental agility

To take another perspective on softness, life is most powerfully represented by a newborn baby, supple, soft and responsive. In absolute contrast, death is a rigid, unmoving corpse. A flexible, responsive body tends to project vitality, openness and aliveness. These qualities can also be applied to thinking. In the modern lexicon, it is viewed as having a *growth mindset*. This is where you demonstrate an openness and curiosity to learn, you are happy to explore new possibilities and are willing to not always have an answer on call. The *fixed* mindset is essentially the opposite to this, where one defaults to known positions, is reactive and is reluctant or closed off to exploring new ways of doing things. The immediate connection with softness and *flow* may be a little opaque here. Consider the fixed mindset as *firm* and rigid, whereas the growth mindset is flexible, agile and willing to yield. Fortunately, the emerging Generation Z are learning the value of having a *growth mindset* as this concept is now taught as part of the school curriculum.

Water always serves

A fertile river basin, a warm bath or a stagnant pool, water always takes the lowest point and from there, serves. Its nature is to nourish, to support, incubate and give life to life. In the actual creation of life, it is a vital facilitator.

Reflect for a few moments on your level of contribution to those close to you and to the world in which you live. Would you gain by expanding the level of contribution and service you offer to others?

> *I don't know what your destiny will be, but one thing I know: the ones among you who will be really happy are those who have sought and found how to serve.*
>
> Albert Schweitzer (Humanitarian & Philanthropist) – 1875

Deal with what is present

This idea relates to dealing with what is as opposed to how you want things to be. When you fail to deal with 'what is', you are avoiding reality and acting contrary to flow. The principle at play here has to do with acceptance. Accept things as they are – including when it is very ugly, challenging or going in the opposite direction to that which you had planned. This approach is appreciated by the military, where there exists the axiom, *all planning goes to naught once the first shot is fired.* Instead of trying to pursue the plan, or follow the theory, you must deal with what is before you regardless of how contrary it is to what you want or expect. Once you have taken this step of truly embracing what *is*, things may change in a more constructive direction. Putting in excessive effort to attempt to avoid or change a situation is contrary to flow. You may get to where you want to be, but in doing so, have you missed better opportunities?

Don't push the river

When you are facing something which has scale, power, momentum and is following its course, as a river does, don't try and push it. You can't and you will be swallowed up or rolled over by the greater energy field. This situation could refer to taking on a task which is beyond your ability to control, particularly if you are lacking experience or resources. The Eastern philosophy of wu wei or flow is as much about conserving energy as it is in expressing it. See things for what they are – a river cannot be pushed.

Clarity of intent and non-attachment

The story which follows is a simple one, highlighting an experience I once had with a seagull, a piece of bread, some unruly emotions and the interplay between attachment and intent.

Years ago, I attended a course which proved to be a real turning point in my life. At lunch, on day three, I walked to a nearby park just off Elizabeth Street, Sydney and began to eat a sandwich. I was feeling raw and vulnerable – just as the program had intended.

As expected, I was soon set upon by the local chapter of the seagull fraternity wanting to muscle in on my meal. More from frustration than kindness, I began to flick them parts of the crust. As I did this, I noticed one of them had a broken wing and was struggling to get some bread as it was hemmed in by its more agile brethren. I felt for this wounded, vulnerable bird and focused my endeavours to provide it with some nourishment. The harder I tried however, the bread pieces kept disappearing under a scramble of squawks, wings and beaks. I kept trying, different angles, different velocities, nothing was working. I was getting angry at my inability to get this bird a few crumbs. Across the road, the gong went off, signalling the resumption of the workshop. Lunch was over and I had to return to face more of my unintegrated self. I stood up, with one last piece of bread resting on my thumb, and casually flicked it, without aim, or attention, towards the mauling mass of feathers. Out of the corner of my eye, much to my delight, my wounded friend, timed its launch perfectly and snatched this last piece of bread out of thin air.

So what?

I am a strong believer regarding the potency of *intent* – where you focus your mind, on what outcomes and for what purpose. The times in my life when I believe I have been successful, there has usually been a very clear *intent* guiding my actions. When I have had my failures, there has been a comparable lack of intent and frequently, too much attachment to specific outcomes.

I believe when excessive emotion is present – anger, fear, guilt, sadness or desire to name a few – there is a high probability this level of energy may act to derail whatever you are intending or hoping to materialise. I cannot prove this perspective beyond anecdotal experience. In applying this theory to my seagull story, I had a clear intent to feed that wounded bird. Crystal clear. However, as my attempts kept failing, my frustrations correspondingly rose. When I had to leave and return to the course, as I stood up, my energy field changed, and I let go of the emotion. This was not a conscious decision, it just happened as I shifted my *attention*. I was not even looking at the bird. When I flicked the final fragment of the bread, my intent still held, but my actions were not impacted by excessive and unnecessary emotion. On reflection, I realised I had lost the emotional *attachment* to feeding the bird which resulted in my original intent being fulfilled.

Tip

In regards to this seagull story and wu wei, there are two aspects to consider. The first is clarity of intent. When you get really clear about an action you want to take or an outcome you wish to achieve, you are focussing your *intent*. With this intent or idea *seeded*, you can step into life, sensitive to those currents or winds, or opportunities, that will be supportive of this intention. Also assisting this process is your internal antenna which filters data and information. It will be attuned to pick up information that which will support the realisation of your intent.

A second point: with clarity of intent, you have moved beyond the potential limitations or restrictions caused by the involvement of excessive emotion. With too much fear, frustration, anger or excessive need to achieve something, to prove something or to get approval, the chances of your intent or your goals being achieved will be diminished. The power of such strong emotions can interfere with experiencing flow because they absorb considerable psychic energy.

Remember, you cannot be genuinely non-attached to an outcome, if you really want it, or need it, to happen. You can't trick the Tao.

Immerse yourself in the experience

There is joy and flow when you allow yourself to engage with something for the sheer pleasure of the experience, without any need to achieve something. In the East, the real value of practising an art such as karate, tai chi, ikebana, calligraphy or yoga is not focused on an outcome, but more on the actual engagement with the activity. Though there are obvious quality benefits – such as with karate, you gain fitness and learn how to defend yourself, with ikebana, you create exquisite art and with yoga, you become healthier and more flexible – to a genuine student, these do not represent the real source of motivation. It is the total immersion in the activity, mirroring the flow state of the West as researched by Csikszentmihalyi.

A story about effortless action

> *Life can be only understood backwards: but it must be lived forwards.*
>
> *Soren Kierkegaard*

I wish I had known of this quote five years ago when I was sitting at Manly Wharf seriously angry after having been told by a colleague I had missed out on a major contract. I had been previously assured this contract was mine. It entailed eighteen months of quality work with a top-tier firm. The previous day I had visited this firm's corporate headquarters to simply 'rubber stamp' the contract. Well .... the rubber didn't hit the stamp and the contract went to a friend. Of course, there was no additional frustration there! As I sat there brooding, my inner script writer began spinning out a storyline, featuring me as the 'victim'. I was deep in the swamp of *Life is not fair*.

Three weeks later, my vexations long gone, I received a call, requesting my attendance at a meeting to discuss possible work opportunities. This was with another fine company and though excited, I kept the lid on any expectations. I went on to win the contract which ran for over four years – the largest piece of work that I have had the pleasure to undertake. The simple truth – had I secured the first contract I would not have had the bandwidth to take on this much larger offering.

Looking backwards, as Kierkegaard's quote suggests, I finally began to understand that weeks before, there had been flow in my life, but I had been insensitive to its subtle ripples. I had been taken by the tide and it had a different destination in sight to the one I had become so attached to. This is the part of the *current* that intrigues me, that aspect of flow which happens whether you are conscious of it or not. Securing the second, larger contract proved effortless, it came to me. And in my understanding, this was a clear expression of wu wei. Effortless action.

This may sound a touch pretentious, as if I am reading too much into it, or simply a convenient explanation of what could be viewed as good luck. Or there could be an even more cynical view, New Age psychobabble! Either way, something which is indisputable – 'stuff happens' – and this stuff proved to be a great gig. Do I think the universe arranged itself to provide me with this contract? No! Therefore, was it just good luck? No. I don't think that either. In attempting to explain such events, which in this story could be termed as 'causality', I am drawn to wu wei and how it does its thing.

Effortless action does not mean you put no effort in. In my case, I have put plenty of effort in over the years. Educating myself, pursuing opportunities and doing my best to deliver quality outcomes. My simple mantra to self, regarding my work, is to ensure I add value. After the frustrations of losing the initial contract had subsided, I withdrew for a brief period and reflected on where my life was and what was important. One thing was clear. Due to my responsibilities, I needed to make money. I felt confident I could achieve this. I was experienced and had a good reputation in the market. I decided however, not to force things. I did not chase after clients, nor shake my network tree and see what fell out or embark on a marketing campaign. I decided not to push against the tide but allow it to come to me and see what it would bring. When it did arrive, with a wonderful opportunity afloat, I was ready.

Reflecting on this period of my life, I believe the calm that followed my initial tantrum, and the fact that I had surrendered any sense of attachment to career outcomes, proved helpful in how my life unfolded at this juncture. I felt a sensitivity to the ebbs and flows of the currents within me and within my life. Fear and anxiety didn't affect me to any degree. I felt a quiet confidence in my own skills and capability. I was clear as to what needed to happen, but not attached as to how this would occur. Like my earlier seagull story, my intent was clear, but I was not attached to how it would materialise.

A suggestion. Engage with these principles of effortless action and non-attachment. Identify an area in your life, where you *really*, really want something specific to happen. Keep this intent clear, i.e., what it is that you want to happen, but let go of all the emotion and expectation you carry, and step back from it, instead of pushing hard towards it. See what happens. Watch and wait and see what the tide or the trade winds bring.

Tip

In closing this chapter on the Tao, a suggestion follows.

Is it difficult to experience the Tao? No! Next time you are near a beach, on a day that is quiet and the waves gentle, enter the water, relax your thinking and lie there, allowing the water to support you. Sense the swell of the ocean beneath you, feel it hold you, feel the current gently take you. Surrender to the sensation of being part of something far greater than yourself. You will experience that 'motion and spirit' Wordsworth was describing in his poem, 'which rolls through all things' for it will be rolling through you.

If there are no oceans, rivers or lakes near where you live, find a place in nature where you can sit still and experience the interconnectivity of the life round you. Observe the multitude of life forms, the colours and tones of nature, the subtlety of sounds and the eternal dance of the elements – of fire (the sun) air, water and earth – fused into everything you see, hear and feel. Just find your inner stillness in such a setting and the Tao will reveal itself to you.

Chapter 15: Zen

There is no other way of life than this way of life.

Zen Master Shunryu Suzuki

Being in a state of Zen and being in flow are one and the same. So, what is Zen? Our starting point to answer this question, is to define what Zen isn't.

> *Is neither a system of ideas, nor metaphysics, nor religion. It is not encumbered with dogmas, nor with beliefs, symbols, temples or monastic vows. In Zen there is nothing to seek, nor any merit to be gained. There is no way, no faith is required, no savior is awaited, no paradise is promised; no choice is offered, nor any attainment.*[1]

If this is what it isn't, then what is it? The following story may help. The acclaimed English philosopher Allan Watts, during a lecture, once paused and held a chalkboard duster in the air. He then asked the students in attendance what was in his hand. Some dutifully shouted back "a duster", to which he responded, "duster .... is a sound". He was demonstrating the limitations that language has in describing the nature of objects and in the larger context, reality itself. Through language we create 'labels' such as a 'duster', but in applying such a label to an object, we do not really capture the true *reality* of that object. Nor would a thousand words, for even beyond its subjectivity, it is impossible for language to fully and effectively articulate and describe 'reality' and what is within it. This is a central theme which permeates Zen.

Having highlighted the limitations of language, I will now (with a nod to the irony) do my best to use language to explore Zen. For example, "*How would you describe the taste of sugar?*". Obviously, you can't to any effective degree, you have to *experience* the taste, to fully appreciate the sensation. So it is with Zen – it is something you have to experience. In practising pursuits such as meditation, martial arts or other art forms such as ikebana, calligraphy or the Japanese tea ceremony you may be fortunate to find, stumble upon, or at least have glimpses of, the pathless path of Zen. Some have found this *path* previously and fortunately have been able to translate Zen in a manner which makes the teaching accessible to the Western mind. A German Philosophy professor named Eugen Herrigel was one such being. In 1948, he published the classic *Zen and the Art of Archery*, which describes his encounters with Zen masters, Japanese archery and the *Way* which has no *way*.

Herrigel's poignant writings trace how he manages to both *find* and lose himself through studying the Japanese art of archery, called kyudo, under the tutelage of a Zen Master. Over a period of disciplined study, he slowly gained the insight that the real purpose of archery is not to hit a target – in other words, achieve an outcome – but substantively more than this. According to his Master, '*By letting go of yourself ... leaving yourself and everything of yours behind you, so decisively, that nothing more of you is left but purposeless tension*'. This is what Herrigel had at first to interpret and then demonstrate. And to fully appreciate this *'artless art'*, his Master further explains that he must become *'simultaneously the aimer and the aim, the hitter and the hit … an unmoved centre'*. The use of such metaphorical-laden language reflects the difficulties of attempting to explain that which is inexplicable.

For a moment, place yourself in Herrigel's geta or sandals as he is practising his kyudo. How would you feel if a revered Zen master stood beside you and requested that, as you draw back an arrow, you *leave everything behind* so that *nothing more of you is left*. Would you think – *'yeah, cool, no worries, got it!'*

Such instructions are obviously metaphorical, and ultimately defy rational grasp. You can't respond with logic or reason, nor philosophical musings – the state he is referring to is beyond the reach of these approaches. The only way is through the physical experience, the immersion which comes from practising the art. This was the path Herrigel doggedly stayed upon and ultimately the practice of kyudo became his meditation on purpose and being. He eventually finds his centre and experiences himself as no longer separate from the action itself. He, along with the bow, the target and the actions of setting, aiming and releasing the arrow, all become a singular expression in time. An experience which represents a poignant and very personal experience of both Zen and the state of flow.

Zen has its origins in Buddhism and has been in Japan since the 12th century. This path was not just for the seekers of enlightenment, from wherever they may emerge, nor monastery dwelling monks or scholars. Many have been drawn to its stark and austere teachings, including the fierce samurai. From the 13th century onward, there was a gradual acceptance and adoption of Zen by the samurai. Zen acted as a guiding path to serve, both in terms of their physical training as well as their spiritual development. This 'Way' or path aligned naturally with their approach to training which sought to identify the most direct routes to 'truth'. In this context, 'truth' stood for the efficacy of a sword strike as much as it related to uncovering the hidden or veiled nature of reality. They lived a lifestyle where death was an everyday possibility, so reflections on spirituality, purpose and existence held a particular and vital poignancy alongside learning the most effective ways of wielding a sword.

> *In Zen there are no elaborations, it aims directly at the true nature of things. There are no ceremonies, no teachings: the prize of Zen is essentially personal. Enlightenment in Zen does not mean a change in behaviour, but the realisation of the nature of ordinary life. The end point is the beginning, and the great virtue is simplicity.*[2]

These lines (composed by the translator) introduce 'A Book of Five Rings' written by the most renowned samurai of them all, Miyamoto Musashi. Like Lao Tzu, in the final period of his life, Musashi retired to a cave and wrote his legendary text, just prior to his death. This book is held in the highest esteem in many parts of Asia and the West and is used by individuals ranging from seekers of spiritual truth through to highly ambitious corporate executives seeking strategic insight and advantage to guide them to their next successful acquisition. His writing style is direct, intense and lacks embellishments – no doubt similar to his fighting style. Paradoxically (which is very Zen), Musashi sought truth and meaning through constantly engaging in contests where a violent death was a very real possibility. In sixty such battles, which have been recorded, he killed all of his opponents. Death was his very close companion. The samurai's pact with their own death is reflected in the opening lines of the book '*Hagakure*', by Yamamoto Tsunetomo, which has been enshrined as their spiritual guide;

The Way of the Samurai is found in death.

Now, for your average hedonistic Western optimist, that is going to sound a bit of a downer. Those living in modern times, wrapped up in their doona and slippers, lounging on sofas and numbed out by TV, would probably have difficulty identifying with such a way of life. So, what relevance is there today in this austere, warrior code of ancient Japan?

The major lessons lie in two areas; exploring how engaged we are with life and, secondly, how conscious we are as we navigate through our day-to-day existence. A samurai's life was enhanced by the very acceptance of death that could happen any day, any moment. This immediacy with death brought forth a unique appreciation and engagement with life. They certainly learned how to *engage with fear and find their flow*. Their existence was purposeful and focused, underpinned by an ultimate raison d'etre – to protect their Lord with their life, or if necessary, die in the attempt. This responsibility brought with it a need for rigorous, daily training, a heightened sensitivity to their environment and a willingness to charge into the heart of a battle at a moment's notice. Due to this ever-present threat of death, life itself became a precious, daily experience. Artistic expression flourished amongst their ranks in such fields as poetry, painting and rituals associated with Zen such as the tea ceremony. In the process of mastering these more genteel arts, the samurai were able to draw upon the mental conditioning and training techniques honed during their training sessions and actual battle.

A guiding principle in sword fighting, as well as in Eastern art, is simplicity, nothing extraneous. Simplicity and efficacy were sought and valued in both the martial arts and creative arts; the swift thrust of a sword, the clean release of an arrow, the impeccable positioning of a flower or the deft stroke of a brush on rice paper. To achieve such potent focus and efficiency took years of dedicated practice. In battle, life was determined by actions taken in microseconds. Too quick for mental processing, movements had to be guided by instinctual impulses bedded-in over years of harsh training. Shifting from the battlefield to the *Way* of the artist, a similar process was required. Artists, then and now, who seek to capture reflections of Zen, need first to go beyond their conscious processing and access the deeper currents of their unconscious. From this state, the artist can paint with a spontaneous freedom, and bring forth the flowing, beautiful and uncomplicated images so familiar in Zen art.

The capacity of Zen to be experienced in such divergent art forms as those of the sword and brush, has helped broaden its appeal to many seeking a spiritual heartbeat and guide in their life, particularly those who are not drawn to the more conventional and structured world religions. There is a distinct lack of dogma to complicate the psyche of a seeker of Zen. Zen has no Saviour's name to uphold, nor to die for, nor to kill for, no commandments to follow, no belief system to defend – ultimate truth, according to Zen, can be experienced by just being present, in life as you are living it. This perception is reflected in the quote by Master Suzuki, which opens this chapter;

There is no other way of life than this way of life.

You may ask ... *that is well and good, but how can this teaching or practice be of any benefit to me here in the current day and age, with no samurai schools to enrol in, lords to protect or battles to fight?* And that is a good question. Taking a key theme from Zen, seek to simplify your life! A potential place to start is to declutter your living environment first and then move on to your mind. Marie Kondo, Japan's organising queen, would be a great teacher to help with the home environment. Influenced by Shinto philosophy, she encourages people to keep that which *sparks joy* in life and quickly and completely discard the rest. After this blitz on your living environment, move onto your mind and start to declutter all those outdated mindsets and beliefs that have gone beyond their use-by-date.

A famous Zen teaching refers to one's life as being like a 'knotted rope'. The knots represent restrictions and complications in life and a student of Zen is advised to seek to 'untie' them and avoid adding to them. When the knots have been released, the rope returns to its *original* nature. As a metaphor, this knotless rope is highly relevant in context to the ever-growing complexity of our modern world. Quality questions to ask oneself are: what knots do I need to untie, where is my life unnecessarily constricted and if I can find a way to pare everything back, what *is my true nature?*

Zen practice does not take you away from the everyday nature of existence in order to experience enlightenment or satori*, but the reverse. It embraces the very mundane activities of daily life as a way to find your own inner truth. Zen embraces the very ordinary activities of life, for when we remove all the definitions, projections and explanations, the ordinary then can become extraordinary.

> *Before enlightenment, chop wood, carry water.*
> *After enlightenment chop wood, carry water.*

---

*Satori is a Japanese Buddhist terms which refers to an 'awakening' or momentary enlightenment. Like a flash of inspiration, an insight arrives which brings illumination.

For adherents of Zen, this immersion in life's daily activities – *chopping wood and carrying water* – includes regular practice of some form of discipline. Whether it be meditation, calligraphy, martial arts, ikebana, the tea ceremony or some other skill, a regular practice provides a way to help control the mind through the discipline and consistent application of attention. In the West, this could be experienced through regular swimming, cycling, gardening, painting or other physical or creative pursuits. This is the *chopping of wood* which quietens the mind and shifts it to the still backwaters and away from the need to be constantly 'on' and in control. The Japanese culture has much to offer in this area. Their lifestyle is rich with examples of where rituals are applied to everyday life as a means to soothe and reduce the undulations of anxiety commonly found in large populations.

My personal experience of *chopping wood* and *carrying water* has revolved around four decades of karate – a study which began in my late teens. I was at university studying humanities when I first stepped inside a dojo and immediately experienced an overwhelming sensation of coming 'home'. I trained for hours every day, loving what I was doing, without really understanding why. I needed no external motivation, for I had surplus within. During these years I read a huge volume of books on Zen and Eastern philosophy as I was determined to find my version of enlightenment or at least hit satori on a few occasions. I failed to comprehend the irony in the Zen teaching, *if you seek it, you shall not find it.*

My seeking was on overdrive. Enlightenment! I wanted it by lunch time. I threw a lot of meditation at it, grew my hair and my face was framed in a Cat Stevens beard. I dressed in loose, monk-like clothes and practised wise and knowing looks. I also had access to a supply of Zen koans at the ready to impress when an opportunity appeared. I maintained my rigorous training, kept reading up on the East, studied philosophy and engaged in a lot of cool conversations at parties and pubs – but still no satori came my way. I was left with myself, an overflowing bookshelf, a collection of quasi hippy clothes and an assortment of deep, spiritual sayings.

On reflection, I look back very fondly to these years and have learnt to suspend judgement of my 20-year-old self. At this age, that seeking, that unbridled, imperfect questing for meaning and truth, is exactly what a young person should be doing.

There were times during these university days when I just abandoned myself to hard training alongside my great friend and mentor, Tony Carroll. We would regularly train ourselves to near exhaustion, and it was during sessions like this, that I would unintentionally experience different states of awareness. Not some grandiose illumination, more just a quieter internal shift in awareness and glimpses into altered states. I believe these experiences occurred due to the level of exhaustion I felt. My body just gave up any sense of rigidity or resistance. The normal physical, emotional and mental sinews which kept me together were loosened and because of this, I had experiences which were out of the norm. At times like this my karate flowed, helped on by the intense exhaustion I felt and the relegation of my ego and inner critic to the back bench of my psyche. It was like my body, psyche and spirit, would all merge into the movement and I would just become an expression of energy in motion.

I only fully appreciated this state of experience afterwards, for had I been 'appreciating' it as I was doing it, there would have been separation between body and psyche. This was not intentional; it just happened that way. I am cautious to label this as Zen, but these experiences have served me with the realisation that there are deeper and more nuanced levels of consciousness beyond the everyday operating level of existence. These moments of inner stillness can be reached, even in the midst of physical movement such as in practising a martial art, attracting for some, the apt description of 'moving Zen'.

Observe a masterful dancer, musician or martial artist in full flight. You can describe what you see with such adjectives as elegance, grace, beauty, power ... but there is something else present, some elusive quality, which is difficult to articulate. This 'quality' can be seen in great art which captures your attention. You stay as if waiting before the painting or sculpture or whatever expression it is, to reveal its secret, a secret which has kept you standing there. But it never does. Language cannot explain it. And that is key to understanding Zen. You never can fully capture, nor describe, what is before you. Or what you are experiencing. As in life, try to clearly describe a butterfly, or the sense of walking on the edge of a beach, in the early morning, as the waves roll in and the sun slowly emerges over the horizon. The essential quality of the experience is beyond the scope of language to fully and appreciatively convey. And this is the space where Zen, through its use of 'koans', toys with our intellect and messes with our absolute reliance on rational thinking and language to define reality and establish 'truths'.

A koan is a paradoxical anecdote, question or riddle, which has no definitive answer or solution. It is intended to help students of Zen gain insight or even flashes of satori, by demonstrating the limitations of language as a means to describe reality or abstracts such as 'Truth'.

An example: *What did your face look like before your mother and father were born?*

The value of the koan rests in its capacity to rattle the rational mind of a student. In their attempt to answer the koan, a student must sort through logic, personal belief systems and their own version of cosmology to arrive at a response. Such challenges are considered helpful for a student wishing to walk the *pathless path* of Zen as they help prepare them to explore beyond the limitations of their own mental conditioning.

I am certain that over the centuries koans have provided much mirth for Zen Masters and at the same time, a lot of grief for their struggling students. A favourite Zen story of mine relates to a student who rushes up to his Master and with a great sense of joy proclaims; *"Teacher, I have gained enlightenment. I have come to realise that there is no reality ... nothing really exists!"* On hearing these words, the Master picks up a large piece of wood and hits the student vigorously around the head. Feeling hurt, the student cries out in anguish. His teacher responds; *"If nothing exists, where did the pain come from?"* The student may have been onto something here, however. According to Louise de Broglie, the great French physicist, electrons which make up the universe are nothing more than a field of possibilities – (*that is a statement worthy of a reflective pause*). This description of a 'field of possibilities' reflects the concept of the great Void, which according to Eastern teachings is where we have all emerged from and in death, will return to.

If there is a recognisable baseline in Zen, it lies in appreciating the value of routine and ritual. This means the 'chopping of wood and carrying of water'. Consider Ikebana, the Way of flower arranging. Though the outcome of arranging flowers may result in a beautiful, aesthetic creation, the real value has been achieved via the 'doing'. This refers to the realisation of a sense of inner harmony and stillness brought about by the quiet periods of contemplation required to select, shape and position the flowers. The intrinsic value to be gained therefore, lies not in a specific outcome, but *through* the experience which has been undertaken to achieve that outcome. A question: Where do you experience stillness in your life? Is it in meditation, time in nature or possibly through some creative or artistic expression? Do you experience enough stillness in your life? I believe an outcome in exploring Zen is the realisation that for many, having more stillness in their life would be of significant benefit. Just being able to detach from the external pressures of life for a short while and find a place within where you can find your version of stillness and rest there for a while.

Don't just do something, sit there!

Buddhist saying

A story: Ikigai – A reason for being

Years ago, I was coaching a young man who was being groomed to take over the family business. This was a law firm which his great grandfather had created and had been passed down through the generations to finally arrive in his lap and as part of his destiny. The problem was, he did not want to be a lawyer. His passion resided elsewhere. That was in designing and building wooden boats. Working hands-on with beautiful timber was both purposeful and soulful for him. He was experiencing a great challenge, being torn between these powerful forces of tradition and the expectation of his family on one hand, and on the other, the draw to where his heart truly lay. He chose boat building and went on to become a very happy and fulfilled individual. My observation was that he understood, appreciated and valued his 'true nature'. He knew where his centre was and the direction in which his own internal compass was pointing. In following this, he was aware of the downside implications. Great upheaval, family recriminations and a strong sense of guilt would follow. But in taking ownership of his life, he was also cognisant that this pain, guilt and sense of dislocation would eventually pass. And when it did, he would be left with his passion and his path before him and most importantly, he knew that he had been true to himself. In making this decision his life became far more simplified, focused, and enjoyable. His courage enabled him to move beyond an impasse, beyond guilt and past the sense of being stuck in the wrong place, doing what he didn't want to do. In simple terms, he unleashed his life and allowed it to travel in a direction which was personally fulfilling. His version of *'chop wood, carry water'* had to do with handcrafting beautiful boats.

The story of the lawyer turned boat builder is an example of what the Japanese call Ikigai. This refers to a pursuit or a practice in life which leads to a 'feeling of accomplishment and fulfilment that follows when people pursue their passions'.[3] The word 'iki' refers *to live* and 'gai' *reason*. As is common with translation, there are many other subtleties, however, in this case the core idea refers to; having a sense of purpose for living and being motivated by that purpose. In the preceding story, when the lawyer turned from a path of law and moved towards where his passion lay, he was aligning himself to the essence of ikigai.

Though ikigai is a very old concept, deeply embedded in the Japanese culture, it has had something of a recent emergence and flowering in the West. There have been many books and articles written in recent years on the subject and a common theme among these works is the connection between ikigai, longevity and the island of Okinawa. Okinawa has one of the highest rates of centenarians per 100,000 people (i.e. individuals living over 100 years of age) compared to the rest of the world. There are many factors attributed to this achievement such as: a very healthy and natural diet, living in a subtropical climate, exercise, social connectivity, psychological wellbeing and low stress levels and a common theme, ikigai. People feel their lives to be purposeful and they are motivated by this. A recent documentary on the Okinawan village of Ogimi, which is world-renowned for its percentage of centenarians, showed how the older people in a village helped look after the local children, even though they were not related. This was an enjoyable, rewarding act of social contribution which was just a norm for this village. When the elders gathered, they enjoyed not only the company of the children, but also one another. In these exchanges, it was evident how much they laughed, exercised and connected. In my own travels to Okinawa for karate instruction, I was struck by just how happy the people are, how respectful they are to one another and just how connected their lives are to the ebb and flow of life around them.

You may be thinking ikigai is an interesting subject, but what is the connection with Zen? This lies in the engagement with the 'ordinary' on an everyday basis – the various personal versions people have of *chopping wood and carrying water*. These simple daily tasks – looking after children, gardening, walking in nature, etc – continually provide the opportunity to experience Zen.

Part of the beauty of Zen is that it transcends the literal interpretations of language and can be found wherever one looks – whether it be in poetry, a painting, in the midst of a dance or a curling wave or even in a quiet moment of solitude. You do not need to be studying some esoteric art form to experience Zen, nor sign up for years in a Kyoto Monastery. You have probably had Zen experiences often and just haven't labelled them as such (which is kind of Zen anyway) just doing the dishes, going for a walk, sweeping the leaves. Zen is wherever you find yourself. These beautiful, lyrical lines concerning the wonderment of life and reflective of Zen, were voiced by Crowfoot, a Blackfoot warrior in 1821, as he lay on his deathbed;

> *What is life? It is the flash of a firefly in the night. It is the breath of a buffalo in the wintertime. It is the little shadow which runs across the grass and loses itself in the Sunset.*

Chapter 16:
The geometry of conflict

We sit around in a ring and suppose But the Secret sits in the middle and knows.

Robert Frost

This chapter explores the martial arts, flow and Zen from a different angle. Literally. We are about to explore Eastern wisdom in the context of geometry.

Interactions between people, particularly in a conflict setting, can be described in terms of geometry. When you take a confrontative position against someone, *you square off with them*. When you direct anger at someone, you *round* on them, attempting to drive *home your point of view*. Alternatively, instead of venting anger, you could take *a different angle*. When you need to reconnect with someone you will *circle back to them*. You may even reflect on some decisions you have made and *come full circle*. In decision-making you will hopefully be *fair and square*. If not, you eventually may need to *square things away*. Otherwise, you may get caught up in a *vicious circle*. Hopefully not involving a *love triangle*. If this happens, you may be forced to move in *other circles*. Quite possibly, you may be forced to go back to *square one*. These are just a few examples of colloquial phrases which are common in our lexicon. You may be thinking, what is the *point* here? This answer lies in this next set of exercises which use geometric patterns to explore communication and conflict.

And before we progress, I would at first like to acknowledge the work done in this context by the Aikido Master, Thomas Crum.[1]

When conflict arises, people tend to take on a shape – primarily in terms of an attitude but also frequently in their physicality and how they express themselves through body language. This dynamic is well appreciated in the martial arts.

When individuals are stubborn and belligerent or just intent on holding their ground, this approach or position can be likened to a Square. When they need to aggress in a focused and deliberate manner, this energy is like a Triangle. Sharp, focused and penetrating. As a balance to both the square and the triangle is the Circle. The strength of this shape lies in its agility and capacity to flow.

So what?

The *central idea* here relates to viewing these geometric shapes as metaphors to help guide how you respond constructively to confrontation or conflict. Conflict usually generates fear in some form and these patterns can be useful as a means to quickly 'shape up' a response. When would assuming the energy of a square be helpful, when do you need to focus your energy like a triangle and achieve cut-through and when, like a circle, do you need to show up with an attitude of openness and adaptability?

The following paragraphs explore how these shapes can be expressed in both a balanced and imbalanced manner.

Square Energy

Square

In Balance: Strength, stability, holding fast, resilience
Out of Balance: doing nothing, resistance, rigidity, stubbornness

Square energy – in balance

When you set boundaries and 'hold your ground' you are expressing the energy of a square. Strong, rigid, dependable, just like old square-like castles from the Middle Ages. In karate, there are specific stances which are intended to help you weather a storm of attack. These stances have you low to the ground, centred, with your feet and toes strongly gripping the floor. They are known as 'square' stances – *shiko dachi*. In life, there will be times when you need to draw upon this type of energy as a shielding and protecting force, particularly if you are leading others. You may be required in tough times to *'have their back'* or be *willing to square up* and support and defend others when necessary. There will be situations when you are required to hold your ground from unfair encroachments on your boundaries. Or, it may also be required when you are standing solid, behind a cause or an individual you believe in. Parents invariably need this square energy on call when they are being assailed by all forms of moods, requests, expectations and aberrant behaviour emanating from their offspring.

In times of crisis, the reputations of leaders are frequently enhanced by the way they acted rock solid and dependable in the face of great challenge. The opposite is also true, where leaders have their reputations shredded by abandoning their people and directing their attention to their own survival. Stories such as these surfaced after the GFC and have remained in circulation since due to their memorable impact.

There will be times when you need to bunker down and approach situations from the protected position of the square. To stop and pause before critical decisions are made or when courage is required to hold one's ground and say what no one else is willing to. In Australia recently, where the Royal Commission steam-rolled through the Banking and Financial Services Industries, the *call to action* had long been voiced by some very courageous whistle-blowers who in their own way, held their ground and called out the many highly unethical and at times, criminal practices inflicted upon thousands of customers throughout the country. They were castles, places of sanctuary for the vulnerable – this is the square energy at its best.

Square energy – out of balance

Imbalance of this energy occurs when its strengths are overused or applied in situations where they should not be. Too much square and you run the risk of being perceived as *being a square,* stubborn or belligerent. As well as this, rigid, unyielding and resistant to change. This relates to the *positions* or *stances* you take in either your professional or personal world as well as the *attitudes* and *mindsets* you frequently default to. There will be times when you will need to give up your *position* and yield to become more triangle-like or circular. In constantly assuming a square stance or attitude, the individual needs to be aware they are running the risk, like the unyielding medieval castles of old, of being bypassed and finding themselves irrelevant.

Triangle Energy

Triangle

In Balance: Focus, clarity, having a point, penetration, edge
Out of Balance: Too penetrating, too sharp, too driven, combative

Triangle energy – in balance

The triangle energy is most appropriate when you really need to focus energy and create impact. This can be in situations where obstacles are met, progress is thwarted and something *penetrating* is needed to shift an impasse. This shape is also highly effective when a vibrant source of energy is required to start something or to drive an initiative forward. The way Steve Jobs drove his career is a quintessential representation of this shape. In organisations which are overly consensus-driven, often what is lacking is this shape. And that is the capacity to make decisions and then to follow through with a focused intent.

Elevating this exploration to a macro level, you can observe how these geometric shapes are reflected in strategy. During the latter part of World War II, the Supreme Commander of the Western forces, General Eisenhower, had a *very square strategy* when it came to defeating Germany. His approach was to advance slowly and cautiously on a very broad front, hold this line, consolidate, and then gradually progress the frontline forward. His subordinate, and arguably the most brilliant of the American Generals, George Patton, was very triangular with his strategy. He wanted to end the War quickly with a concentrated effort of massed forces against a narrow front. This represented what would have been a very deliberate thrust into the heartland of the Nazi Germany. Eisenhower's approach prevailed, Berlin was left to the Russians to conquer, and the map of Europe reflected this in 1945 and stayed that way till 1989.

There are times when you need to cloak yourself in your warrior apparel and draw upon the triangle to express focus and have impact. This is when you need to get things done, cut through, and create momentum. The story of Alexander the Great and the Gordian knot, whether it is true or not, or a mixture of fact and myth, powerfully illustrates the utilisation of the triangle energy. As the story goes, there existed a prophecy, foretold by an Oracle, that whoever could untie the Gordian knot – a tightly entangled series of ropes which had apparently no start or end point – would be the future King of Asia. Alexander, through his successful battles, eventually got to stand before this 'knot'. At first, he began to try and untie it, but eventually seeing the futility of this, drew his sword and sliced it in half with a single bold stroke. Reasoning that it would make no difference how the knot was loosened. The gates to the city opened and before him, Asia beckoned. As with Alexander, there will be times in life, when a singular action is required to 'cut through'. This is the strength of the triangle energy – edge, focus and drive.

Triangle energy – out of balance

We have all been on the receiving end of this type of energy. As with squares, the virtues of a triangle – sharpness, pointedness, penetration, cut-through and decisiveness – used in an excessive manner, or in an inappropriate way – creates damage. Excessive assertion can be experienced as aggression or bullying. In conflict situations, this can relate to actions undertaken or words spoken. People long remember when they have been wounded by the excesses of someone's forceful nature, unrealistic demands or *pointed barbs*. Self-awareness is critical in assisting you give shape to how you show up.

Circular Energy

Circle

In Balance: Flow, blending, harmonising, engaging, inclusive
Out of Balance: Indecisive, lacking focus

Circular energy – in balance

When you approach a situation, either in a conflict or otherwise, with an attitude of curiosity, openness and flexibility you are expressing the energy of a circle. When you don't have a fixed point of view and are willing to ask questions and be influenced by the thoughts of others, you are demonstrating that wonderful capacity of flow. Circles don't have sharp points, nor are they rigid like a square and they can move either towards something or away from it without causing collateral damage. Showing up with a circular energy is also more likely to create a sense of psychological safety for all who are present. The energy of a circle is a good place to begin a communication or engagement as you are open, receptive and capable of flowing with what transpires. At some point your view may narrow and sharpen and then you may be better served by being more triangular or square.

Circular energy – out of balance

Nothing in excess is carved in the walls of the forecourt leading to the entrance of the Temple of Delphi, dating back to ancient Greece. This statement sits beneath the more famous maxim, *Know Thyself*. When applied to circular energy, *nothing in excess* is indeed a wise warning. If there is too much circular energy, you will fail to get traction and go in circles, wishy-washy like a whirlpool. This can be experienced in the professional world when you have teams or organisations which are overly consensus-driven and leaders who are hesitant or too timid to take over and make decisions. This builds frustrations in the ranks and cries of, '*I just wish they would make a decision and get on with it*'. This frustrating interplay can also be seen in dynamics involving family or friends, where, faced with a decision, everyone is too polite to make a call.

When required, you do need to have an edge. People who are overly circular in their way in the world are frequently driven by a need to be *all things to all people.* This approval-seeking behaviour is prone to backfire and end up causing frustration as there will be a lack of clarity, decisiveness and direction. As mentioned in the previous paragraph, showing up with circular energy is a great place to initiate a conversation but at some point, the transition to either a square or triangle may be required.

So what?

In any day of your life, in any given situation, be it a meeting, an exchange in the corridor, a presentation or a phone call or email, you may be well-served by consciously choosing one of these three shapes to guide how you will show up. The trick is knowing what shape will serve you best in what situation and at what point you need to shift your shape. You could approach a conflict situation all circle – open, responsive, curious – and then quickly find you need to defend your boundaries, for your openness is not reciprocated and you realise you require a square-like response.

For others who are accustomed to using positional power to get what they want, they may find in these changing times, that the forceful, triangle energy, has diminishing utilisation as people are less willing to be on the receiving end of excessive assertion or bullying. During any exchange between people, you could see all three 'shapes' being expressed in how people are communicating. Being able to adapt and utilise the strengths of the shapes when most appropriate is the key point here.

Consider two people meeting, both showing up with the triangle energy as represented in the diagram that follows. When it comes to 'dialogue' there will be two points colliding, leaving very little in terms of space for discussion or negotiation. One, at least, needs to yield and become more circle-like. They need to roll adjacent to the other triangle, to get their viewpoint, their perspective. They need to shift from a point of view to a different *viewing point*. If they go square, then whoever has the greater authority will tend to prevail. The square will resist the triangle attack. Or, if the person expressing triangular energy has the authority, then she or he will dominate. With peers interacting who hold the same level of power, there needs to be some circular energy. This will show up as a willingness for one, or both, to yield from their position and move towards the position of the other. If there is an impasse, then voluntary movement by one to shift to a circle approach, will help break this. This dynamic is expressed in the diagram below.

Exercise

Try this – next time you are confronting a difficult situation, arrive as a circle. Begin by being open and curious and not holding a 'position'. You may need to adjust to more triangle or square during the exchange, but the circular approach is a good place to start to set the tone for the conversation.

Case study

A highly visible expression of *circular* energy was on display during South Africa's Truth and Reconciliation trials which started in 1995. These were established to help the nation heal the wounds of apartheid and move forward as a genuine democracy. The focus was on reconciliation, not revenge. Open hearings gave opportunity to both victims and perpetrators to tell their story, with many of the perpetrators eventually granted amnesty. It was an incredibly courageous and radical approach by the political and legal hierarchy of South Africa, and it yielded profound results. Had the Courts taken a more triangular approach and been driven by a punitive philosophy, there may have been very different outcomes and more than likely, a slower more intractable journey towards national healing.

It is easy to write off such a concept as these shapes as something quaint, impractical or far too abstract to be of any real utility. In working in countries around the world, delivering a broad range of topics and skill training, this exercise – Square, Circle and Triangle – has been one of the most popular and well-regarded. On revisiting many of these places, or on follow-up coaching calls, what has been most evident is how well-utilised this tool has been. I recently overheard a conversation between a very senior leader in a consultancy firm, who knew of this material, and a junior associate he was coaching. He was giving feedback to the associate regarding his style with clients. He explained that his approach to the client had been way too triangular. He mentioned how the associate had kept trying to drive his point home (and the sale) to a reluctant client. He then went on to explain the virtues of having a circular approach to start with, and to fall back to.

Tip

Others do feel the weight and type of energy you bring into a room, onto a screen or to a conversation. The tip here is to be conscious of *how* you want to show up and what energy you want to project. These three broad categories – square, triangle and circle – can act as quick, back pocket reminders to help you shape up, how you want to show up.

The value of having straight lines in your life

A final piece of geometry – the straight line. A karate sensei once said to me that *discipline gives freedom*. This struck me as quite an intriguing statement and I was curious about the element of contradiction within it. He went on to explain that having a discipline – as in the martial arts, yoga or athletics, or in an artistic expression such as music or art – is like having a straight line in your life. The discipline creates the straight line which acts both as an anchor to ground you as well as a compass to guide you.

With these lines (disciplines) in place, the rest of your life can unfold and dance around them, for you have these anchor points which ground you. Without these straight lines to give you stability, you may be more vulnerable when the winds of life blow fiercely. With a lack of anchor points, your life can drift aimlessly and whilst this maybe attractive for a while, eventually you may find yourself without direction, lacking purpose and a long way from tapping into that which is shining deep within you. In studying the lives of people who have truly excelled, whether in artistic, sporting, scientific or business worlds, their capacity to draw on discipline is a common denominator.

Chapter 17:
A model to remember: CCE

The work I have been involved with over the last three decades has included the use of many models. By 'model' I am referring to frameworks used to synthesise and symbolise constructs, ideas, tools and teachings. The iceberg analogy referred to in earlier chapters is one such example. I have avoided packing these pages with too many models for my intent has been to focus on a few key ones. With this approach in mind, I present you with this final model which I hope – a touch like the One Ring in *'Lord of the Rings'* – will act to bind the key teachings and ideas presented in this book together in a way which is efficient, effective and memorable. The model is positioned here to help synthesise the set of skills we have been exploring – mindfulness, presence, centredness and ultimately flow.

CCE model – Centre, Choose and Engage

This model is intended to help you simplify and shape your response to a challenging situation.

Step 1. Centre

Something happens, a stimulus of some form occurs. Examples could include a request for your help, a situation where a conversation suddenly heats up, or even a threat appears in some form. Whatever it may be, you need to respond. The first step is to centre yourself (as represented by the dot – or still point – within the circle). Remember to breathe into your hara, putting your hand there if it helps. Or maybe just think *hara* and breathe in a deep and calming manner into your lower belly. In doing this, you have caused yourself to pause, become present and, by breathing into your centre you will begin to feel focused, mindful and energised. The sensation of feeling centred can be achieved in seconds by this simple approach. Being centred will prevent you from making a rash, poorly judged response to the stimulus before you.

Step 2. Choose

The next step is to choose your response. The circle symbolises being open, curious and exploratory and this mindset provides a good place to start shaping your response. You are taking an *active* position, shaping up a response in the moment, and not just habitually defaulting to a well-worn, previous pattern of response. Depending on the situation, this pause could be for as long as needed, or if an immediate response is required, just long enough to discern what that response needs to be. A shorthand response could be guided by taking either a circular, square or triangle approach.

Step 3. Engage

A quick recap. Something has happened, which requires you to respond. You have paused and centred yourself as in Step 1. You have identified a response, as in Step 2. And now, in this final step, you need to initiate your response – you need to engage.

Responding as a **square** energy could look like you are holding your ground, determined not to be pushed around or overly influenced by others and you are hesitant about moving too fast or too far forward. There is caution with the square and a need for stability. You feel centred and confident and feel no need to be reactive or overly excited.

Responding with the **circular** energy is about being open, curious, willing to experiment and not holding a fixed position. With circular energy, comes a lot of questions. This is a useful place to initially engage with others for it helps create understanding and trust and provides insight for what is required to confidently create your next steps. There is a vitality in the circular energy and certainly a willingness to move, explore and develop.

Responding with the **triangle** energy is about being energised, assertive, focused and having a strong position or a point of view. This energy is often required when things get stuck or there does not appear to be any form of leadership or direction taking place. This energy is also helpful when you are feeling the need to have an impact and get things happening.

So, next time you are confronted by a challenging stimulus of some form, try using this model **CCE. Centre** yourself, **choose** an appropriate response and then **engage**.

Chapter 18:
A few thoughts about luck

Here's the thing about luck... you don't know if it's good or bad until you have some perspective.

Alice Hoffman

"I don't think I'll take the medal as the minute and half of the race I actually won... I'll take it as the last decade of the hard slog I put in."

Steven Bradbury – Olympic Gold medalist

I find the notion of 'luck' perplexing. Whether luck is 'good' or 'bad' is completely contingent upon what variables have been selected including the time frames. What has 'good' and 'bad' luck got to do with flow? Individuals who rejoice in their good luck and blame bad luck for their woes will fail to sense the currents of flow in their life. If you believe you are but a leaf, blown about and buffeted by the visitations of 'good' and 'bad' luck you will fail to appreciate the agency you have in being able to shape and influence the trajectory of your life. *A story to illustrate this.*

Insights gained after being shot

When I was fourteen years of age, my best mate, Col, shot me with a .22 rifle, firing a hollow-point bullet, which came to a resting point deep in my upper thigh. The backdrop to this event was a simple camping expedition. We had just set up our tent, helped by Col's two young nephews, when a large black snake slithered past us and entered a nearby water hole. Col grabbed his rifle and shortly after was aiming at the snake. I was watching from across the other side of the billabong, completely in his line of fire. Just as a flat stone will bounce off water, so will a bullet if the gradient of the trajectory is not too acute. He pulled the trigger, the shot missed the snake, bounced off the water and it hit me, opening quite an entry point, as hollow-point bullets are designed to do.

Col and I now faced a serious problem beyond me being shot. We were a pair of trespassing, underage shooters, with unlicensed rifles and we had just committed a dangerous act in public. The Authorities were a definite concern, but not nearly as scary as Col's father – Col Senior. A very tough, no-nonsense bushman with a leathery face and equipped with long, sinewy and very powerful arms which had been shaped by years of hard, manual work. Things were not looking good for Col Junior. Self-preservation required us to concoct a story. This tale of teenage subterfuge, created by an increasingly nervous Col Junior, followed a storyline that I had been hit by a ricochet off a tree and my leg, now doused in Dettol and covered in band aids, had just been grazed – an explanation which is reasonably plausible to country people. The problem was, as we spun the story to both families, we hid the fact that I still had a bullet deeply lodged in my leg. I kept this minor detail quiet and pushed back concerns now surfacing about blood poisoning and infection, because one backs their mates in the bush.

Many hours later, I was finally home, dropped there by Col Senior. He stayed and engaged my father in a long conversation regarding the perils of shooting, particularly the risk of ricochet. Not long after he left, I noticed my slippers filling with blood and realised I needed to 'fess up'. The Dettol and band aids were not quite best practice when it came to a bullet wound. I eventually spilled the full story, telling my father, that there had been no ricochet, but a deflection and that my leg had now become the final resting point of this bullet. This was around fourteen hours after being shot. I was taken immediately to the hospital, knowing that I was in for some more pain, but nothing compared to what I knew would descend upon my doomed mate. On reflecting on this event years later, I am still stuck by the comic moments caused by a pair of fearful teenage boys trying to cover their tracks, dodge the Authorities and most importantly keep Col Senior well away from the truth.

When I was recovering, post operation, many people offered opinions regarding what and why this had happened. These observations invariably involved either good or bad luck. Some would opine – *It was simply just bad luck that I had been shot*. No, it was not bad luck – I was dumb, positioning myself in the line of fire. Physics happens. Others would comment – *I was lucky it hit me in the upper thigh and not some other more vulnerable place, like my groin*. No, I was not lucky. A few centimetres to my right and the bullet would have missed me completely. *So, if that had happened, it would have been good luck?* No – chances were, it could have hit either of his two young nephews who were standing next to me at the time, both of whom came up to my hip height. If it had struck them in the head, it would have killed them. *Oh ... in that case it was good luck it hit you then*.

I rest my case on luck – it depends on what variables you choose.

Good luck vs bad luck: another story

An old farmer was talking to his neighbour one day, leaning on the rails of his stockyard. They were looking at a herd of wild horses which had recently been caught by the farmer's son.

The neighbour said, "Fine horses. Such good luck to have captured these animals and not costing you any money".

The old farmer reflected for a moment and replied; "Good luck, bad luck, who knows, life knows. See the lead stallion there. My son tried to break him in, but he was too powerful. He threw my son in his first attempt to ride him and when he fell his leg was broken".

The neighbour was surprised and replied; "Wow, that was bad luck".

The old farmer was quiet for a moment and then replied; "Good luck, bad luck, who knows, life knows. Remember several weeks back, when the army recruiters came through to enlist the young men from the village to fight in the big siege near the city. All our local boys were either killed or injured in that battle. They didn't take my son on account of his broken leg".

The neighbour responded, "He was so fortunate. Such good luck".

The old farmer paused longer this time before replying; "Good luck, bad luck, who knows, life knows".

So what?

If you were to refrain from pointing to good luck when things happen fortuitously for you and not blame it when the reverse happens, would the level of personal accountability you hold for your life be increased? And if this happened, would you feel a greater sense of control and balance in your life? And if you assumed accountability and felt more in control and in balance, how would that impact your life?

Another perspective to view events in one's life is through the lens of karma. Does it exist? It certainly seemed to, in the context of my experience of being shot. I had to recover from a painful bullet wound, Col Junior received an almighty belting from his tough father when the truth of the story finally emerged, and the snake, unharmed in any way, got to move on with its life.

Chapter 19:
The hero's journey

The Journey undertaken by a seeker of higher truth, is a symbol that binds, in the original sense of word, two distinct ideas, the spiritual quest of the ancients, with the modern search for identity.'

Phil Cousineau

' ... we are the victims of academic, scientific, and even therapeutic psychology, whose paradigms do not sufficiently account for or engage with, and therefore ignore, the sense of calling, that essential mystery at the heart of each human life.' [1]

James Hillman

The central theme in this book focusses on meeting fear head-on and engaging with it in a manner which deprives this emotion of having an exaggerated level of power over your life. To achieve this outcome, this guide strongly suggests a series of disciplines and techniques involving learning how to be present and centred, as well as encouraging you to explore the benefits of the flow state as put forward by both Western and Eastern teachers. As fear loses its capacity to restrict the full expression of who you are, or the life you are leading, options multiply and new pathways emerge.

You – As the hero, in your own life's journey

The questions that follow are intended to inspire reflection on the potential directions your life could take and what possible journeys you could embark upon in the years to come.

📖 Exercise

If you had more courage, what would you be doing that you're not doing now?

_____
_____

What is something substantial that you would really like to do with your life at this current point in time? (*NB You may have answered this in your response to the first question.*)

_____
_____

What is the first step to take to move towards this?

_____
_____

What action could you take to ensure you commit to this initiative?

_____
_____

No doubt this idea or initiative has already whispered to you in some form – maybe on the edge of your conscious mind or in your dream state. New adventures always begin with a call of some form.

This call, according to the mythologist, writer and scholar Joseph Campbell, is what heralds the initial stage of the *'hero's journey'*.

Campbell, who made his life's work studying and decoding myths from all around the world, garnered fame for, among many substantive achievements, being a key inspiration behind George Lucas's creation, 'Star Wars'. Those who study his writings can easily identify that the path that Luke Skywalker ventured on is a clear representation of the hero's journey.

The value in exploring the hero's journey lies in its capacity to be an instructive metaphor, as well as a guide, for your own life. For ultimately your life is heroic. Most of the time we fail to appreciate this however! You may be thinking – *As I am sitting here in my ugg boots and tracky dacks watching reruns of Breaking Bad ... in all honesty... my life doesn't feel all that heroic.* So, allow me to convince you otherwise.

Life has an entry point called birth and an exit point in death. In between, there exists a path full of lessons to be learnt, challenges to be overcome, adventures to be embarked upon, victories to be secured and all manner of emotions and experiences to be lived. Like the questing Knights of antiquity, you will have to confront dragons on your path. These exist in the substance of your physical life and show up as bullies, backstabbers, belligerent bosses, manipulators, charlatans, players and all sorts of tricksters. They are self-serving, potentially dangerous and do not hold your wellbeing as a priority. They will test you, hurt you and ultimately teach you a lot about yourself and the world you live in. There are also dragons that inhabit your inner world. They are your fears, self-doubts and self-destructive behaviours. They cause chaos, unhappiness and pain and bring limitations. Like Ged, the wizard of Earthsea, you need to be able to name these elements and control them, otherwise they will control you. The upside to these difficulties which assail the traveller on the hero's journey is the offering of great opportunities, personal transformation, gifts and adventure and most importantly, growth and nourishment of the Soul.

Prior to delving into what the hero's journey represents, some context is required. The universal theme of a hero, travelling on a perilous path, seeking some Grail, treasure or reward is well-embedded in Western literature, as it is, in the Western psyche. Odysseus, Beowulf, Hercules, Boudicca, King Arthur, Joan of Arc, Frodo, Luke Skywalker, the Karate Kid, Harry Potter and Daenerys Targaryen are all stories representative of this construct. In real life, we have great exemplars such as Neil Armstrong, Nelson Mandela, Jessica Watson and Malala Yousafzai – the Pakistani schoolgirl who survived being shot by the Taliban as a punishment for pursuing her call, which was the promotion of education for girls in her homeland. The call is not just for the high-born, or for the warrior caste, but for all of us.

Like the hero in so many of the great stories, you too will answer *calls*. In doing so, you will be required to let slip the moorings of your own comfort zone and venture out on quests to expand the boundaries of who you are. You will learn much about life, you will earn gifts, meet wise ones and ultimately have opportunities to transform your life. And because of this, you will add value to others in the process. If you reflect on your life which has already passed, there will be *calls* you have answered. *Calls to Adventure,* to commitment in relationships, to career, parenthood, education, travel, service and self-development to name just a few areas where these *calls* arise.

What is the hero's journey?

During his decades of intense exploration into myths, Joseph Campbell became fascinated by the frequency in which so many stories shared common themes, characters and structure. Preeminent among these patterns is the storyline of the 'hero' (representative of both genders) being called to action and required to undertake a challenging quest which, if successful, will be both personally transformative and beneficial for others. The quest is an act of service, helping others – his or her family, the village, tribe or nation. The gifts or boons the hero secures such as fire, healing powers, or something specific like the Golden Fleece, the sword Excalibur or the Arc of the Covenant, are the rewards for the courage, tenacity and skill they have demonstrated.

On hearing a *call* the hero is usually reluctant at first. After a period of hesitation passes, the hero eventually summons their better angels and responds to the call. This signals the beginning of the adventure. The arc of the quest which follows, is ultimately transformative, allowing the 'hero' to discover strengths and skills to which they were previously blind. This trajectory is clearly evident in the film 'Star Wars', where we observe Luke Skywalker, slowly awakening to the powers within him – a development caused by his need to confront the mounting calamities which threaten to overwhelm him.

This central idea of a hero, questing on a challenging journey, in service to others, is a concept still very alive today. We see it in literature, movies and in real life. Everyday citizens, responding to some call to action. In recent years, the courage demonstrated by firefighters in Australia has been epic, as has been the front-line medical staff around the world in their incredibly daunting and life-threatening task of attempting to save vulnerable people during this pandemic. These are courageous acts of service, undertaken ultimately for the benefit of others and often at an extreme risk to those responding.

Stages of the hero's journey

According to Campbell's research, the Journey is divided into three distinct stages – Departure, Initiation and Return.

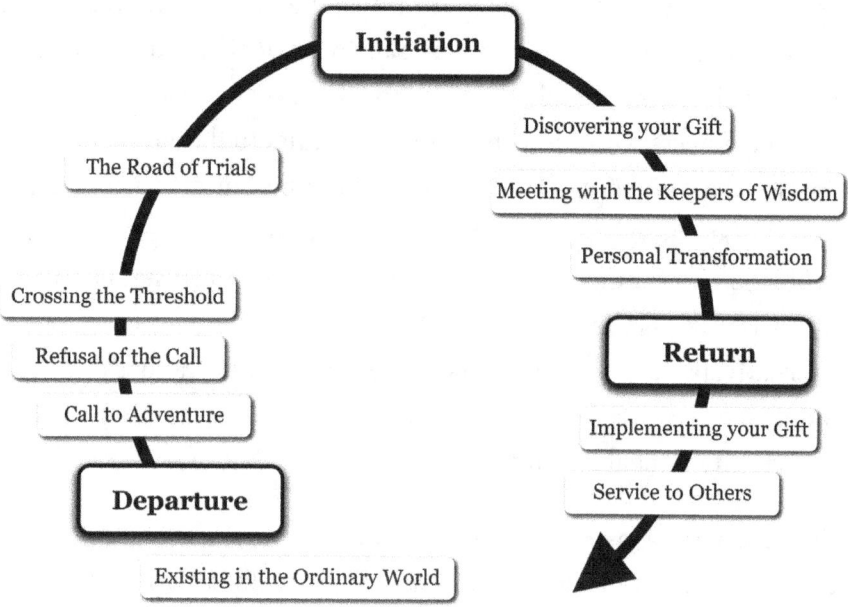

Each stage has several **sub-stages** where there are various challenges to overcome and tasks to be achieved. The initial stage of **Departure** begins in the everyday, or *Ordinary World* where life follows its normal routines. This predictability is broken by a *Call to Adventure* where something intervenes to act as a catalyst to move the reluctant hero out of the ordinary, daily patterns of life – possibly a new job offer, an overseas trip, a spark of creativity hits or the stirrings of a romance. *Refusal of the Call* frequently follows. This is where the hero frequently experiences hesitation and fear and becomes more sensitive to the cold, threatening edge of their comfort zone. This proves to be an inflexion point for many, where a multitude of reasons – usually driven by fear in some form – emerge to justify a *Refusal*

of the Call. This could show up as *a new job offer being rejected, a great opportunity ignored, or a promising romance stalled.* Effort is then directed towards a rapid return to the routines and comfort of the known life. The psyche has been disturbed however, and the soul awakened by the sense of adventure the *Call* has offered and as a result, the *Ordinary World* will fail to quell this impulse once it has stirred. Courage is finally summoned, fears overridden, and the hero reconnects with his or her mojo, commits to the *Adventure* and *Crosses the Threshold*. This crossing could be initiated willingly, or it could be caused by a 'mistake' or a 'stumble'. Odysseus steered right when he should have rowed left, and fortunately that happened otherwise '*The Odyssey*' may not have been such a rip-roaring story. Alternatively, it could be life itself, booting you in the backside and out of your comfort zone. For others, the call may come as a profound opportunity to heal a wound.

The next major stage is **Initiation**. This pivotal phase of the Journey embraces the sub-stage of the *Road of Trials*. In the trials, the hero must confront numerous tests, on many levels. Both outwardly in the physical world and inwardly, having to face inner 'demons' showing up as fears, self-doubts, self-loathing and other vulnerabilities. *The Road* is often fraught with danger but also rich with great opportunities for growth and learning. As examples of this phase consider Steve Jobs in his quest to start Apple and Jessica Watson, solo sailing around the world at sixteen. In this phase, strengths need to be discovered and 'owned' by the hero and brought to the battle. The symbolism here is very powerful and these inner, previously unrecognised or discarded qualities don't necessarily refer to the ability to wield a mean lightsabre. They encompass a very much wider breadth of attributes such as self-belief, confidence, courage, wisdom, intuition, guile, creativity and willpower. The *Discovery of these 'Gifts'* is a reward for the courage the hero has demonstrated in answering the *Call*, surviving the *Road of Trials* and by being willing to learn from the sages and wise ones that move in and out of their epic journey offering wisdom and guidance; just as Athena did to Odysseus and no doubt, just as some mentors have done for you.

Throughout the *Initiation* stage, the hero undergoes a baptism of fire in some form of challenge or multiple challenges. Think of Hercules. He didn't retire to Santorini after dealing with the Nemean lion. The analogy here – when confronted with a raft of challenges, to prevail, you will need to draw upon additional strengths and skills that you are either unaware of, have disowned or ignored. The severity of the challenge requires you to reconnect with and 'own' these innate qualities.

So, what is the relevance of this section, Initiation, for the average citizen like myself who heads off to work each day, confident I won't be attacked by a posse of Orcs or imprisoned in a cave by a one-eyed giant?

Quality question! As we have been observing these stages of the Journey, hopefully you have been able to make some transference from the world of myth to your everyday life, particularly dealing with fears and self-imposed limitations. Fears are like dragons from the great stories. You can't run from them, they are too powerful – you need to confront them, like the heroes from the great myths, with courage, skill and guile. Fears can be highly impactful and if held over a long period of time can certainly sabotage one's life. Fears associated with relationships, career, creativity, dealing with addictions, self-loathing and other crippling self-inflicted vices can act to inhibit a more expansive and true expression of yourself. Courage is required to embrace the talents, skills and creativity you have been blessed with and bring these into the light. As Nelson Mandela stated in his inauguration speech;

It is our light, not our darkness which most frightens us... Your playing small doesn't serve the world.

In addition to the gifts which are bestowed, the *Initiation* aspect of the Hero's Journey, includes the sub-stage, *Meeting with the Keepers of Wisdom*. This stage witnesses the arrival and contribution of mentors and wise ones. Athena, Merlin, Gandalf, Yoda or in more contemporary terms, Master Shifu, from Kung Fu Panda, represent powerful exemplifiers. Who have been your *keepers of wisdom*? School teachers, coaches, loving relatives or older friends? What tends to identify mentors, apart from their wisdom, is a capacity they have, to see more in you than what you see in yourself. Also, their acts of service, support and love come with no strings attached. Which is a rare thing.

After *Initiation*, the final stage, **The Return** opens before the weary hero. This witnesses their return to their family, tribe or nation, bearing gifts of power such as Arthur's Excalibur or the bounty of fire as in our First Nation's aboriginal myths. The completion of their journey revitalises their people through these gifts, but the real value is imparted through what they themselves have learnt and by *who* they have become. This is the personal transformation they have been forced to undergo to survive the rigours of their quest. This transformation may show up as the emergence of emotional qualities such as being more courageous, caring, intuitive, generous or loving. Or the journey may have engendered other qualities such as the capacity to lead, or to be creative, imaginative, inspiring or gifted with the ability to heal. The qualities Luke Skywalker gradually recognised within himself during his *Trials* is a classic example of this transformation. This is not referring just to the Force, but to other qualities such as courage, loyalty, guile and the self-belief which he eventually embodied.

The Return is the crowning aspect of the Journey. Without it, the path that has been taken is not a true heroic journey and the travellers not heroes as they are more likely to be motivated by self-serving and egotistical motives. This is clearly seen in the twists and turns of Lance Armstrong's very dramatic rise and fall from heroic status. But like us all, his journey is incomplete and as Bob Dylan sings *'this wheel's in spin'*. Who knows what ultimate direction his life may take?

The Hero's Journey in film

You do not have to look far to find clear representations of the hero's journey as it is a very common theme in books, poetry, and most pervasively, the cinema. A contemporary story which clearly demonstrates the overall architecture of the hero's journey is *'Jerry Maguire'*. And of course, the hero… Tom Cruise. The value in exploring such stories is that they are our modern myths which permeate this present world and act to guide us – both consciously and unconsciously.

Jerry's *Call to Adventure* follows an epiphany he has regarding the manipulative and mercenary nature of the business in which he is employed. This insight leads to the realisation that his career, as it is currently unfolding, is slowly destroying him. Instead of leaving the industry, his *Call* is to transform it from within. He pens an inspiring, values-based Vision and Mission Statement, only to have difficulty trying to recall it the next day when fear steps in. This action represents his *Refusal of the Call* as the realisation sinks in just how far he has launched himself out of his comfort zone. He has now stepped too far out from what had been his life. As he arrives at work the next morning, the scene frames the lift shutting behind him, symbolically representing his former life has ended. He has bungled his way onto the *Hero's Journey* and his life is about to be rapidly enveloped by a plethora of challenges as he reluctantly and unwittingly hits the *Road of Trials*.

These *Trials* see much of what he has striven to achieve in his life crumble rapidly. He is left battered and bruised with little dignity, gravitas or money. His only real supporter is an empathic PA and a solitary athlete, whose star power is on the decline. The traditional trajectory of the Journey now usually sees the arrival or emergence of some form of mentor to help the beleaguered 'hero' re-find their true North. In this story, the mentors that emerge are snapshots of older Sports Agents who keep us informed on how a true, authentic professional should behave. Although he does not hear these musings, he does manage to listen to his own inner voice which acts to guide him through the current train-wreck of his life. This is his gift, his boon. He learns how to lead his life according to his own moral compass. He discovers what is important and meaningful in his life – true love, relationship and connection. He has re-found and returned to his true nature and in doing so, discovered not only genuine love, but also a sense of fulfilment and purpose in both his personal life and career. The beneficiaries of this new-found purpose are his loved ones, his clients and ultimately himself. This is his *Return*.

'Jerry Maguire' has significant lessons embedded in its finely nuanced script. Are there similarities you can identify with? Have you felt the strong pull of your own moral compass, indicating a need to change direction? Maybe you have realised a point in your life or career where you know you need to experience something different, what has previously inspired you no longer does, and you are looking for that next spark. Maybe you have heard the *Call to Adventure* but refused it and have been left uncertain as to whether you made the right decision?

Real life heroic journeys

A contemporary *hero* who represents the hero's journey and deserves recognition for his courage and tenacity, is Eddie Mabo, the Indigenous Australian, born in the Torres Strait, who was pivotal in securing land rights for his people and the wider Indigenous population. His *Call* came in the form of an everyday conversation with an academic at James Cook University where he worked as a gardener. He was casually informed that the land he thought he and his people owned, was recognised legally as Crown Land. This everyday conversation proved to be a turning point in his life. In its mysterious ways, life had just opened a door and offered a *Call to Adventure.* Mabo knew this was their land, always had been, always will be and this fact needed to be enshrined in law. Unlike some heroes in real life, or those created in stories, when he heard the call, there was no hesitation, no pausing at the threshold. He launched into this quest with passion and purpose and was completely convinced of the rightful cause for which he was fighting. This was a fight worth fighting and it was well overdue. Along his *Road of Trials*, he overcame huge challenges, on many levels, in particular dealing with institutionalised racism. He was fortunately supported by many drawn to the cause, which included a collection of motivated and highly competent lawyers who helped him navigate through the perilous straights of terra nullius – a set of antiquated laws;

> 'which defined land which was 'supposedly' uninhabited as liable for government seizure'.[2]

Eddie Mabo died before he witnessed the full outcome of his quest – the overturning of *terra nullius* and the implementation of the 'Mabo decision'. This was a legal framework which introduced the principle of Native Title which recognised Aboriginal and Torres Strait Islander peoples have rights to the land that existed before British occupation. The 'gifts' or legacy which resulted from his inspiring journey benefitted not just his own Torres Strait people, but all Australians. In the redress of these racist and exceedingly unjust laws, a powerful and inspiring step was taken towards genuine reconciliation. And Eddie's story, like journeys undertaken by other true heroes, continues to act as a torch, inspiring others to take up calls to action.

Erin Brockovich was a poor single mother who was struggling to pay bills when her *Call* first sounded. Working as a support assistant in a small law firm, she was exposed to a story of suffering, corruption and an appalling misuse of power. The dragon she was to confront, a soulless corporate giant, soon showed itself. After tremendous struggle and personal loss, she eventually prevailed and won justice for her profoundly affected clients. Though well-rewarded for her quest, the financial outcome was not the motivation behind her actions. This came from a deeper driver imbued with the moral imperative to support people who are vulnerable. She cuts an intriguing figure. Her quest was launched from a small country town in the backblocks of California, a *Call* she answered which was to have a deep impact on her life and many others and yet, at no point could she have foreseen this happening. Her legacy, as with that of Eddie Mabo, is assured.

Reflection

The *Road of Trials* is a journey we have all most likely experienced, many times in many different contexts. These 'trials' may have taken only hours or could stretch out for years. The pivotal learning in these experiences is usually transformative. The Hero, or, your good self, having been exposed to challenging situations, prevails and is strengthened and transformed by the experience. The opportunity which presents when you do answer these *Calls* is to inspire others by what you learn and by what you become. Another benefit which sometimes fails to be recognised, is that your life gets to be reinvigorated.

In a recent interview, Australia's oldest living Olympian, the centenarian Frank Prihoda, was asked the secret to his longevity. His response:

Don't be afraid to take risky situations, go through them and try to do it for yourself. If you sit on your backside and don't do these things, you will short-change yourself and miss out on life's experiences.

Frank escaped from communist Czechoslovakia in 1948 by skiing across a frozen lake to reach Austria, to eventually start a new life in Australia.

Answering the Call

Not all *Calls* are to be answered. There are certainly situations where refusing the lure is the correct response. There are sirens out there singing and when you hear them, unless like Odysseus, you are tied to some form of a mast, wax your ears and don't listen. Some hear the siren's song and just dive overboard to their eventual regret. Others hear the music, but realise it is not for them. Consider some decisions taken, investments made, or situations where you have been too trusting. Being able to discern which calls are to be answered and which ones avoided is a very useful attribute.

Tip

I am hesitant to offer too much instructive advice as to what calls to answer and which ones to avoid. I would suggest if it were a major adventure, before you commit, have some conversations with people around you who have wisdom. Garner different opinions. Be conscious of the dance of your own internal biases. If fear is causing you to hesitate to commit to the call, then really do an internal audit. Are these fears warranted, or am I just anxious about going outside my comfort zone? If that is the case, is it sufficient reason to *Refuse the Call*?

Calls come in many forms. Some are immediate, compelling and exciting. Some point towards great opportunities. Some are to do with things you need to confront. Others are frightening and enticing all at once. Some bang on your doors, some speak to you quietly and others reveal themselves slowly over time. There could be multiple calls and challenges like the Knights from the Arthurian legends, venturing on various quests – to find love, to experience illumination, to discover the grail or to heal a wound. Others may find themselves in the middle of an unexpected journey, thrust there in some serendipitous manner by unforeseen forces of life. A brief personal story follows a *Call* I answered one hot and dusty day which started in a most innocuous manner and ended up completely transforming my life.

A personal story

It was my seventh year as a high school teacher. The school had just completed its annual Athletics Carnival and the teachers, after having been baked in the sun all day, were tired and weary as they filed back into the staff room. My colleague Ross, a middle-aged veteran of the teaching ranks, flushed by the heat turned to me and in a matter-of-fact manner stated; "*Well Peter ... only fifteen more of those Carnivals to go before I get to retire*".

This casual observation hit me like a sledgehammer. I didn't respond for a few moments as my mind slid into some kind of holding pattern. I knew something significant had just happened, but I was not immediately aware of what it was. I took a few moments to pause and reflect on what, on the surface, was essentially an innocuous line by my colleague. The epiphany I eventually had, was that this comment carried some weighty implications for my teaching career. After a long pause, I replied in a humorous manner, "*Well ... That's it Ross. I am out of here... otherwise I could end up like you!*"

At the end of that year, I made good on my word and resigned. I loved teaching for a multitude of reasons but something deep within me, like a siren's song, a positive one in this case, had been playing at the edge of my consciousness for some years. I didn't want to end up like Ross, counting down the days and years until retirement. There was more out there in life that I wanted and needed to explore. Regardless of how rewarding I found teaching, I knew my life needed to move in another direction – but what that was, I had no idea. I felt considerable fear. Leaving a solid, predictable base to step into a void, required courage. Particularly when the self-doubts and a myriad of insecurities, many of which were warranted, made their presence felt. But despite this internal conflict, I knew I had to make that step. This was a Crossing of a Threshold to the next journey of my life. I had to leave one life behind so I could find the entry point to another. I had to embrace my fears and find my flow.

The step I took was highly irresponsible on many levels and I am certainly not putting myself forward as something of a role model. I was married, with a young son Zac, and I was the key breadwinner. We had practically no assets or savings and here I was, resigning from a good and stable career to step into ... nothing... a void. This was one of those situations when I just knew, at some deep intrinsic, inaccessible level, that things would get better and that I would eventually find my true north. I knew I had to leave the boundaries of my teaching career and step into whatever life presented to me. Something out there was calling...

Years of significant challenge and growth followed. I returned to exploring areas where I felt a genuine passion. This included study in areas such as psychology, philosophy, metaphysics and meditation. I enrolled in many courses to do with the human potential movement. At this point my life was a mixture of great learning and growth as well as financial hardship and constant challenges on many levels. We had very little money, so much so that numerous times I was checking under the floor mats of our old car to find out if there was enough money for a coffee. Covering rent alone was a frequent struggle. Despite the financial struggles I was on a *path with a heart* and that was where I wanted to be. To borrow Joseph Campbell's wonderfully evocative phrase, I was following my 'bliss'.

This was a time of my life where both my wife and I were deeply immersed in studying self-development. Ironically, it was also a period which witnessed the breakdown of our marriage. After some painful and jarring experiences, we ended our marriage and made our ways separately to Melbourne to start new lives. Arriving in that fine city, I found myself penniless and hollowed out by the turmoil following the collapse of a marriage and a family life I had been living. This painful confluence of events also coincided with the launch of my new career which was teaching ... self-development! This meant helping others get their life together. The irony did not escape me. Somehow, I managed to function. This was a *Road of Trials* I had not prepared for, nor expected. I was dealing with dragons in every corner of my life, internally and externally. Fears, self-doubts, anger, frustrations visited me daily in barely manageable doses. I was supremely aware of the incongruous situation I had found myself in. Teaching all this great material and obviously not having lived it through my marriage. I was acutely aware of not having walked my talk. My major concern at the time, as with most parents who go through divorce, is for their children's well-being. I was no exception here and I did all that I was able to for my son. The only real upside at the time was that the pain, confusion, bewilderment and fear I experienced greatly enhanced my understanding of the human condition, in particular the power of genuine empathy.

During these years, my life certainly did not feel heroic in any sense. I had made choices which had unleashed a whole range of dynamics which I had no way of foreseeing nor planning for. I just had to learn to surf as the waves kept rolling in. Somewhere within me however there was always a quiet, reassuring sense that ultimately things would work out. At the time, I couldn't point to many areas in my life that would indicate the veracity of this almost subliminal message, but somehow, I knew it to be true.

I kept working in the human potential arena and shifted my focus from teaching public seminars to small corporates and then eventually onto larger corporations. This material embraced areas such as self-awareness, resilience and emotional intelligence, targeted towards helping professionals, particularly leaders, to become more authentic, centred, inspirational and ultimately more effective.

I was kept busy, working in this domain during the late 1990's and eventually began to find a balance in my life, financially and emotionally. I loved the work and felt it genuinely contributed value to people's lives. What I did not see on the horizon was an incredible opportunity this type of work was to offer. An opportunity which, in looking back, has proven to be the most beneficial career step in my life.

This step came in the form of an invitation to join a newly established group within the global consulting firm, McKinsey&Company, called the PLI – Performance Leadership Institute. The company was looking for facilitators who had been working in the areas of emotional intelligence and behavioural change. After an exhaustive series of interviews, I was one of the fortunate few who made the cut and joined a team of wonderful, creative and highly-competent colleagues. I felt extremely honoured and humbled and knew inside that some part of my journey had just experienced a completion and a new one was about to start. Even though I was feeling somewhat awed by the reputation of this company, in particular the exacting standards and extremely high work ethic, I knew this was where I was meant to be. I was in flow.

The next nine years that followed were a blast – an incredible journey through every continent in the world, working with inspired companies, great people, fabulous material and guided by a very clear and compelling purpose. My personal life was also to gain some 'gifts' around this time in the form of meeting my beautiful partner in life, Janine and to be blessed with the arrival of our daughter Jessica just a few years later.

The key person driving this transformation work at McKinsey was a highly talented and inspirational senior partner named Michael Rennie. Michael's very successful career had met a turning point several years earlier when he was diagnosed with cancer. He survived this harrowing experience and, in the process, became determined to do things differently when he returned to the corporate world. In contemporary language, and one intended to be complimentary, he would be termed as a 'disruptor'. He was inspired to bring the awareness he had gained through his experience with cancer back to his colleagues and clients. To achieve this, he became a very passionate advocate for the value of the 'softer skills' in business.

This broad label, popularised by the work of Daniel Goleman, focuses on emotional intelligence which promotes self-awareness, self-regulation and empathy. Aligned to this work, Michael also endorsed the benefits of meditation and mindfulness training which he attributed to helping him overcome cancer. Taking this new wave of skills and practices to the corporate world, with the intention of transforming organisational cultures and making leaders more self-aware and compassionate became Michael's *Call to Adventure*.

As with all bold *Calls to Adventure*, it does not take long until the path taken encounters all sorts of challenges. Practices associated with meditation and mindfulness were very much on the fringe of corporate mainstream at the time and were not given serious attention, particularly by companies like McKinsey, who prided themselves on their data-driven intellectual skills and depth of research. To Michael's advantage, this ability to undertake very rigorous research proved to be propitious. When the company decided to research meditation, the result was a most compelling picture of an extensive range of benefits this practice bestows. This research certainly helped the PLI's cause, but the main reason for our eventual progress and expansion was because of Michael's dogged determination.

I remember with great fondness a story he told us in the early days of the PLI. Our morale was down as we were meeting significant resistance within McKinsey itself and with clients, in terms of the acceptance and uptake of our 'softer skills' approach. In his story, he drew on Schopenhauer;

> *All truth passes through three stages. First it is ridiculed. Second it is violently opposed. Third it is accepted as being self-evident.*

This perspective proved to be highly prescient relating to the core content we were promoting. Twenty years later, the evidence is in – witnessed by the current wide-scale popularity of these topics in business, leadership books, blogs, apps, articles and Ted Talks. These concepts, skills and practices have all become mainstream. This is not to claim this all happened only due to McKinsey. There were many other competent individuals and companies moving in the same direction. However, because of McKinsey's reputation, the championing of such 'controversial' practices certainly helped the extensive acceptance and legitimacy of this material on the global stage. The small, inspired light that first shone in a Sydney office at the turn of the century gradually grew in strength and is still shining brightly today.

In this journey, Michael was greatly helped by Gita Bellin. Gita has extensive experience in meditation, self-development and facilitation. She was responsible for supporting and guiding a cadre of facilitators who could effectively take this contentious material to the heartland of the business world and deliver it with both style and impact. Together they formed an extremely effective, though unusual pairing, which acted as the driving force behind the practice. The work came in slowly at first and then took off like a rocket to all corners of the world.

Fortunately, I was a beneficiary of this journey. Of the many destinations my career took me to, my favourite was always South Africa. I was there from 2003-2008 and it was incredibly gratifying to work in culture change at this time as the country itself was undergoing a nationwide social and cultural transformation. This upheaval was reflected in riveting stories emerging from the workshops in which I was involved. Stories of despair, of extreme poverty, of deep and enduring anger, as well those of love, hope, inspiration and confidence in a better future. These stories are still with me and that is their real gift – stories anchor in both heart and mind and from there continually provide guidance, wisdom and nourishment.

This period of my life spent with McKinsey proved to be my *Gift*, earned from surviving the rigours of a tough and challenging *Road of Trials* and ultimately a reward for answering a *Call* to expand my horizons. The difficulties I had endured and overcome, though minor compared to what some face, had certainly been worthwhile given the compelling opportunity which unfolded before me. The years leading up to this new adventure had been a time of deep and powerful learning, which I have only fully appreciated in hindsight. The years since have made up my *Return* and in the intervening period there have been many other calls to adventure, roads of trials, dragons faced, gifts earned, and mentors met. The overarching *Journey* however, the one which tied them all together, began many years before, when my colleague spoke about his yearning for retirement after spending a hot and dusty day at a school's athletics carnival. That was the spark. That was the *Call*.

And are you aware that *Calls* can come at any time, in any guise? Are you listening?

Fear, flow and the hero's journey

The previous paragraphs capture my *Call to Adventure, Road of Trials, Gifts* and *Return*. What about you? What have your *Calls* been? *Calls* to move on from a comfortable life and go off to adventure, calls to commit to relationships, new business opportunities, career progression, marriage, parenthood, calls to the arts, to sporting pursuits and to spiritual journeys. Not all are to be answered, for that is part of the magic. Listening to your own spirit within, discerning which *Calls* to respond to, and what paths to take, make for an inspiring, challenging and rewarding life. You won't always get it right. Some of my *Calls to Adventure* I responded to have ended disastrously. In avoiding such pitfalls, you need to pay attention to that inner voice of discernment. Knowing when to be bold and push forward and when to pause and catch your breath and review your options, is a true skill. Pausing before you cross that threshold may save you a lot of pain and problems. At times, when facing a crossroads in your life, it is definitely okay to pause, reflect and just maybe, return along the path you have come and see what you may have missed.

The trick is knowing when your fears and apprehensions are warranted and when they are not. If a compelling opportunity is before you, do your checks and balances. If after this exploration, the only real impediment to stepping forward is fear then you should embrace it, thank it for doing its job and engage with what is before you. As Joseph Campbell would suggest – commit to the *Call* and cross the threshold. In this way you are taking ownership of your life and what is before you and not allowing fear to hold you back from the expansive and magical opportunities when they arrive. In doing so you are stepping into the *flow*.

It is natural, when you come to major decisions in your life, that fear kicks in and old, unhelpful stories resurface and re-run in the jukebox of your mind. Many of the fears that emerge in such times, however, have long exceeded their use-by-date. You have just managed to keep them on life support by occasionally giving them airtime and oxygen. This usually comes in the form of an internal narrative which you will know well, as you have heard it many times before. Hit a subject area and out comes the usual, stale stories associated with that theme. Contemporary research detailed in Chapter 3 informs us that with disciplined attention, neuroplasticity gives us the capacity to overwrite or change these stories and write new ones.

There is much substantive guidance on how to move your life forward constructively and creatively. Mr Csikszentmihalyi would implore you to believe in yourself and suggest you seek opportunities where you can develop and immerse yourself fully in the state of flow. In the East, a Mr Miyagi may remind you that if you become present with the moment, the path forward will reveal itself naturally and therefore fear will be unable to find a space to inhabit and fester. A Taoist teacher may suggest when an appealing opportunity presents, be like water and flow into that space. And always remember wherever you take yourself, bring your centre with you.

I will leave you with a favourite saying of mine, told to me by an old teacher.

The meaning of life is what you discover in yourself.

Hopefully, these pages will inspire you to discover the gifts and treasures which lie within you, patiently waiting to be found. And when discovered, they will help you experience greater levels of flow, fun and fulfilment in your life.

Notes/Bibliography

Chapter One

1. A wave ski is a small kayak-like craft you sit upon and steer with a paddle. Real surfers who stand up call such craft 'goat boats', meaning whoever is riding them is a goat. Wave ski riders call surfers 'speed bumps'.

2. Pillay, S.S. (2010). *Life Unlocked: 7 Revolutionary Lessons to Overcome Fear*. Rodale Books. New York p.58.

3. Csikszentmihalyi, M. (2002). *Flow*. Rider. London. p.74.

4. Magrini, M. (2019). *The Brain: A User's Manual*. Short Books. London. p.128.

5. Ackerman, David. (1996). *A Natural History of the Senses*. Phoenix. London.

Chapter Two

1. Goleman, D. (2006). *Emotional Intelligence*. Bloomsbury. London. p.60.

2. Ibid. p.60.

3. Greenfield, S. (1996). *The Human Mind Explained*. Henry Holt & Company. Gordonsville. p.11.

4. Magrini, M. (2019). *The Brain: A User's Manual*. Short Books. London. p.6.

5. Greenfield, S. (1996). *The Human Mind Explained*. Henry Holt & Company. Gordonsville. p.12.

6. Ashwell, K. (2007). *Anatomica: The Complete Home Medical Reference*. Globe Publishing. Ultimo. p.169.

7. Goleman, D. (2006). *Emotional Intelligence*. Bloomsbury. London. p.10.

8. Ibid. p.12.

9. Nichols, W.J. (2014). *Blue Mind*. Abacus. p.50.

10. Goleman, D. (2006) *Emotional Intelligence*. Bloomsbury. London. p.96.

11. Ashwell, K. (2007). *Anatomica: The Complete Home Medical Reference*. Globe Publishing. Ultimo. p.167.

12. Martino, B D. (2010). Amygdala damage eliminates monetary loss aversion. California Institute of Technology.

13. Ashwell, K. (2007). *Anatomica: The Complete Home Medical Reference*. Globe Publishing. Ultimo. p.169.

14. Goleman, D. (2006). *Social Intelligence*. Hutchinson. London. p.273.

15. Ashwell, K. (2007). *Anatomica: The Complete Home Medical Reference*. Globe Publishing. Ultimo. p.169.

16. Goleman, D. (2006). *Social Intelligence.* Hutchinson. London. p.273.

17. Dispenza, J. (2012). *Breaking the Habit of Being Yourself.* Hay House. Sydney. p.99.

18. Wise, J. (2011). *Extreme Fear: The Science of Your Mind in Danger.* St. Martin's Press. New York. p.17.

Chapter Three

1. Bergland, C. (2017). *How do Neuroplasticity and Neurogenesis Rewire Your Brain.* Psychology Today.

2. Ibid.

3. Rock, D. (2020). *Your Brain at Work.* Harper Collins. New York

4. Magrini, M. (2019). *The Brain: A User's Manual.* Short Books. London p.6.

Chapter Four

1. Goleman, D. (2015). What it takes to become a socially intelligent leader. Retrieved from https://www.linkedin.com/pulse/what-takes-become-socially-intelligent-leader-daniel-goleman

2. Ibid.

3. Frankl, V. (1947). *Man's Search for Meaning.* Beacon Press. Vienna.

4. Ibid.

5. Ibid.

Chapter Five

1. Le Guin, U.K. (1972). *A Wizard of Earthsea*. Puffin. Sydney. p.73.

2. Sabater, V. (2018). Exploring Your Mind. The Shadow Archetype – The Dark Side of Your Psyche. Retrieved from https://exploringyourmind.com/shadow-archetype-dark-side-psyche/

Chapter Six

1. Magrini, M. (2019). *The Brain: A User's Manual*. Short Books. London. p.127.

Chapter Seven

1. Hehir, J. (Director). (2020). The Last Dance (TV Mini Series). Episode 10. Netflix and ESPN Films.

2. Hanson, R. & Mendius, R. (2009). *Buddha's Brain*. Hanson. Oakland. p.13.

3. Mindful Nation U.K Report (2016). Report by the Mindfulness All-Party Parliamentary Group (MAPPG). *Journal of Vocational Education & Training*, Vol. 68, No. 1, 133-141.

4. Souter, F. (August 13, 2021). Article – Good Weekend Magazine. *Sydney Morning Herald*. Sydney.

5. Gould, K. (2019). The Vagus Nerve: Your Body's Communication Superhighway. *Live Science Contributor*.

6. Gerritsen, R.J.S. and Band, G.P.H. (2018). Breath of Life: The Respiratory Vagal Stimulation Model of Contemplative Activity. *Frontiers of Human Neuroscience*. Vol. 12, 397.

7. Magrini, M. (2019). *The Brain: A User's Manual*. Short Books. London. p.161.

8. Rubenstein, J.S., Meyer, D.E., Evans, J.E. (2001). Executive Control of Cognitive Processes in Task Switching. *Journal of Experimental Psychology: Human Perception and Performance*, Vol. 27, No. 4, 763-797.

9. Cherry, K. (2020). How Does Attention Work? Theories on Cognitive Psychology. *Very Well Mind*. Retrieved from https://www.verywellmind.com/how-does-attention-work-2795015

10. Dispenza, J. (2012). *Breaking the Habit of Being Yourself*. Hay House. Sydney. p.58.

11. Church, M. (2002). *High Life 24/7*. ABC Books. Sydney. p.20.

12. O'Kelly, E. (2007). *Chasing Daylight: How My Forthcoming Death Transformed My Life*. McGraw-Hill Education. New York.

Chapter Eight

1. Hanson, R. & Mendius, R. (2009). *Buddha's Brain*. Hanson. Oakland. p.44-45.

2. Wise, J. (2011). *Extreme Fear: The Science of Your Mind in Danger*. St. Martin's Press. New York. p 176.

Chapter Nine

1. Seligman, M. (2011). *Flourish*. Random House. Sydney. p.40.

2. Cleary, I. (2015). Neuroplasticity and Anxiety. Retrieved from https://iancleary.com/neuroplasticity-and-anxiety/

3. Clear, J. (2018). *Atomic Habits*. Random House Business. Sydney

4. Harris, R. (2008). *The Happiness Trap: How to Stop Struggling and Start Living*: A Guide to ACT. Trumpeter Books

Chapter Ten

1. Random, M. (1978). *The Martial Arts*. Octopus Books. London. p.236.

2. Fields, R. (1991). *The Code of the Warrior*. Harper Perennial. New York. p.124-125.

Chapter Eleven

1. Legge, J. (2001). *Tao Teh Ching by Lao Tzu (Translated with commentary by James Legge)*. Axiom Publishing. Sydney. p.64.

2. Mondschein, K. (2016). *The Art of War & Other Classics of Eastern Philosophy by Sun Tzu (Introduction by Ken Mondschein)*. Canterbury Classics. San Diego.

Chapter Twelve

1. Wilhelm, R. (1931). *Secret of the Golden Flower: A Chinese Book of Life*. Broadway House. London. p.94.

2. Mitchell, S. (1993). *The Enlightened Mind: An Analogy of Sacred Prose*. Harper Perennial. p.191-192.

Chapter Thirteen

1. Csikszentmihalyi, M. (1997). *Finding Flow: The psychology of engagement with everyday life*. Basic Books. New York. p.30.

2. Csikszentmihalyi, M. (2002). *Flow: The classic work on how to achieve happiness.* Rider. London. p.53.

3. Csikszentmihalyi, M. (1997). *Finding Flow: The psychology of engagement with everyday life.* Basic Books. New York. p.31.

4. Csikszentmihalyi, M. (2002). *Flow: The classic work on how to achieve happiness.* Rider. London. p.75.

5. Csikszentmihalyi, M. (1997). *Finding Flow: The psychology of engagement with everyday life.* Basic Books. New York. p.117.

6. Ibid. p.117.

7. Ibid. p.122.

8. Vasarhelyi, E. C., & Chin, J. (2018). Free Solo. National Geographic Documentary Films.

9. Ibid.

10. Csikszentmihalyi, M. (2002). *Flow: The classic work on how to achieve happiness.* Rider. London. p.74.

11. Vasarhelyi, E. C., & Chin, J. (2018). Free Solo. National Geographic Documentary Films.

12. Csikszentmihalyi, M. (1997). *Finding Flow: The psychology of engagement with everyday life.* Basic Books. New York. p.28.

13. Ibid. p.31.

14. Seligman, M.E.P., & Csikszentmihalyi, M. (2000). Positive psychology: An introduction. *American Psychologist*, 55(1), 5–14.

Chapter Fourteen

1. Hansen, C. (Translator). (2012). *Tao Te Ching on The Art of Harmony by Lao Tzu (Translated by Chad Hansen)*. Duncan Baird Publishing. London. p.7.

2. Mondschein, K. (2016). *The Art of War & Other Classics of Eastern Philosophy by Sun Tzu (Introduction by Ken Mondschein)*. Canterbury Classics. San Diego.

Chapter Fifteen

1. Random, M. (1978). *The Martial Arts*. Octopus Books. London. p.93.

2. Harris, V. (Translator). (1974). *A Book of Five Rings by Miyamoto Musashi (translated from the Japanese by Victor Harris)*. Allison & Busby. London. p.7.

3. Kumano, Michio. (2018-06-01). "On the Concept of Well-Being in Japan: Feeling Shiawase as Hedonic Well-Being and Feeling Ikigai as Eudaimonic Well-Being". *Applied Research in Quality of Life*. 13 (2): 419-433.

Chapter Sixteen

1. Crum, T. (1987). *The Magic of Conflict*. Simon & Schuster. New York. p.136-137.

Chapter Nineteen

1. Hillman, J. (1997). *The Soul's Code*. Warner Books. New York. p.6.

2. Wikipedia. (2021). Eddie Mabo. Retrieved from https://en.wikipedia.org/wiki/Eddie_Mabo

About the Author

Peter is a business consultant, facilitator and executive coach with an extensive experience of working with individuals, teams and organisations. He has worked with thousands of people, across a reach of more than thirty countries, with a focus on unlocking and cultivating human potential. A personal quest, which began in his teenage years, seeking awareness and meaning, translated into his professional career and ultimately found its way onto the pages of this book.

A core element and guiding light in this quest has been Peter's long-term love affair with Martial Arts and Eastern philosophy. He has studied and taught karate for over forty years, achieving a 4th dan ranking in Okinawa in 2017. He currently continues his consultancy work and leads a Shorin Ryu karate-do club on the Northern Beaches of Sydney. He is married, with two children and one recalcitrant cat.

www.petershearerauthor.com.au

www.ingramcontent.com/pod-product-compliance
Lightning Source LLC
Chambersburg PA
CBHW070537010526
44118CB00012B/1158